coolcamping

GLAMPING GETAWAYS

SECOND EDITION

by Andrew Day, David Jones and James Warner Smith

Edited by Martin Dunford

The publishers assert their right to use *Cool Camping*
as a trademark of Punk Publishing Ltd.

Cool Camping: Glamping Getaways (2nd edition)

This edition published in the UK in 2016 by

Punk Publishing Ltd
81 Rivington Street, London EC2A 3AY
www.punkpublishing.co.uk
www.coolcamping.co.uk
Copyright © Punk Publishing Ltd 2016

A catalogue record of this book is available from the British Library.
ISBN
978-1-906889-65-4

10 8 6 4 2 1 3 5 7 9

introduction

Great news, bunting fans: glamping has come of age. Since our first edition in 2011, glamorous camping has enjoyed a huge rise in popularity. Sure, it was already *de rigueur* at many campsites and festivals, but now you can expect to find glamping options at your favourite luxury hotel or your best friend's wedding (as per Guy Ritchie's nuptials). A glamping holiday was even included in the prestigious goodie bag for Oscars nominees, but sightings of Bradley Cooper and Meryl Streep toasting marshmallows by the light of a head torch remain unconfirmed.

Glamping has its spiritual fluffy-cushioned home here in the British Isles. Nowhere else has seen such a groundswell of enthusiasm for the idea of luxuriating in the outdoors, driven both by the explosion of high-quality glamping options and the innovation in the type of accommodation on offer. Of course, glampers can enjoy a night in a yurt or

tipi. But the more adventurous can now try a converted mobile theatre, tree-houses in the woods… or an expertly transformed shipping container!

But is that really glamping? Purists may say that only canvas structures qualify; others that the term only applies to temporary accommodation. We prefer an inclusive approach – tree houses, pods, containers and cabins are all invited to the party, as long as they're a bit special.

New glampers take note: there's a huge variation in the level of luxury on offer from site to site. Some places provide five-star luxury with plumbed-in bathrooms and breakfast in bed. Others simply offer a pre-pitched tent and an air mattress, with the expectation that you bring your own bedding and cooking paraphernalia. So the onus is on you to check that facilities match expectations.

Within these pages you will find an eclectic mix of our favourite glampsites across Britain. The common feature is that they all offer a unique and memorable way to enjoy the great outdoors with minimal hassle, planning and packing. Just consider Glamping Getaways the Oscars of the glamping world. No goodie bag required.

campsite locator

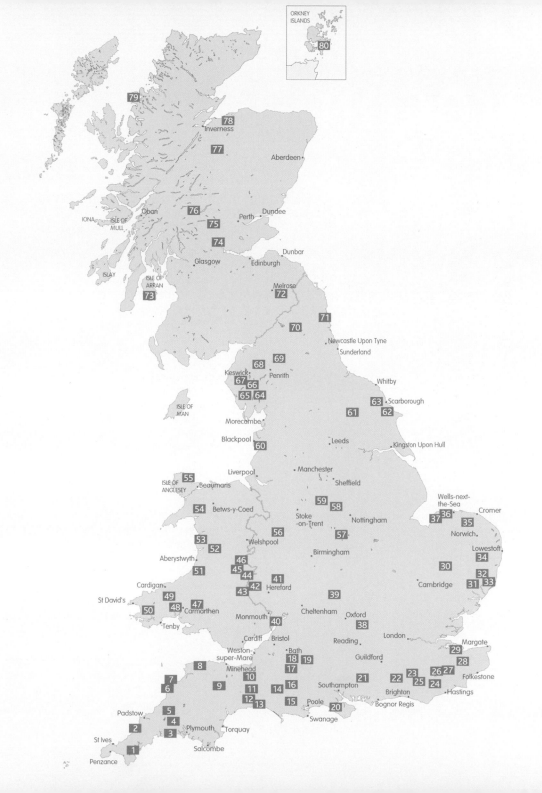

ORKNEY
ISLANDS

80

79

78
Inverness

77

Aberdeen

76
Oban
IONA
ISLE OF
MULL
75
Perth • Dundee
74
ISLAY
Glasgow • Edinburgh
Dunbar
ISLE OF
ARRAN
73
Melrose
72

71
70
Newcastle Upon Tyne
Sunderland

68 69
67 Keswick
66 Penrith
65 64
ISLE OF
MAN
Whitby
63 Scarborough
61 62
Morecambe

Blackpool
60
Leeds
Kingston Upon Hull

Liverpool
Manchester
Sheffield

ISLE OF
ANGLESEY
55
Beaumaris
Wells-next-
the-Sea
36
Cromer
54 Betws-y-Coed
59 58
37 35
Stoke
-on-Trent
Nottingham
Norwich
56
Welshpool
57
Lowestoft
53
52
Birmingham
34
Aberystwyth
46
30
32
51
45
44
31 33
Cardigan
42 Hereford
Cambridge
43 41
St David's
49
39
50 48 47 Carmarthen
Cheltenham
Oxford
Tenby
Monmouth
38
40
Cardiff
Bristol
Reading
London
Margate
Weston-
super-Mare
Bath
Guildford
29
8
18 19
28
Minehead
17
21
22 23
26 27
7
10
Southampton
25 24
Folkestone
6
9
Brighton
Hastings
11 14 16
12 13 15
Poole
Bognor Regis
5
20
Swanage
4
3
Padstow
Plymouth Torquay
St Ives
2
1
Salcombe
Penzance

trecombe lakes

Opened in 2013, Trecombe Lakes is one of Cornwall's loveliest new glampsites. Tucked away in a tranquil waterside spot near the charming village of Constantine, this idyllic setting is perfect for a hassle-free Cornish break. The six pods that comprise the glamping lodgings are perfect for reluctant tent campers. Somehow managing to be both cosy and airy, the fully insulated pods are kitted out with comfy beds (one double and a couple of singles) and linen, so all you need to do is bring yourself and an appetite for exploring this magical corner of south-west England. There's even a cute little kitchenette so you can cook up a storm using some of the fine Cornish produce on offer (be sure to ask about the site's special breakfast hampers) and an en suite toilet and shower room inside each pod. Kids will love exploring the nine acres of woodland and the play area with climbing wall, tree-house, nets and rope swings. The centrepiece of the site, though, is the eponymous lake (sensibly fenced off from the play area). Should you tire of the innumerable places to visit off site (including the path of the nearby Helford River), jump in one of the complimentary rowing boats for a peaceful paddle on the water, before lounging back on your decking with a beer and a barbie on the go. Pure bliss.

Trecombe Lakes, Nr Constantine, Falmouth, Cornwall TR11 5JW 01326 211850 trecombe-lakes.co.uk

❋ Six double-glazed and fully insulated pods, each sleeping 4, with 1 double and 2 single beds (travel cot also available), toilet, shower and kitchenette equipped with electric hob, sink and fridge. Bed linen, bathroom towels and kitchen equipment are all provided. The decking area has a picnic table, outdoor beanbags, a Webber BBQ and firepit. Communal laundry. Woodland play area, boating lake.

❋ Explore Falmouth's maritime heritage and buzzy arts scene or, of course, Cornwall's famous pristine beaches. Maenporth Beach is one of the region's more popular spots yet is refreshingly uncommercial. For something a little more adrenaline fuelled, Lizard Adventure (07845 204040) specialise in kayaking, coasteering and climbing excursions along the rugged Lizard Peninsula. Glendurgan Gardens (01326 252020) and Trebah Garden (01326 252200), both in Mawnan Smith, are two of Cornwall's finest gardens, the latter with colourful exotic blossoms cascading down to a private beach on the Helford River. Enchanting St Michael's Mount (01736 710265) is a tidal island with its own medieval castle, now owned by the National Trust.

❋ Cornish tea and breakfast hampers, brimming with all manner of local produce, are available upon booking. The multi-award-winning Trengilly Wartha Inn (01326 340332) serves up fantastic local ales and dishes. The Potager Garden and Glasshouse Cafe (01326 341258) serves fabulous vegetarian dishes and enjoys a beautifully bucolic setting. The Ferryboat Inn (01326 250625) has been serving pints for the last 300 years: boasting breathtaking waterfront views, it's a truly atmospheric setting in which to enjoy fresher-than-fresh seafood.

❋ Open all year.

❋ Three-night weekend £245–£425; 4-night midweek £285–£485; 7 nights £395–£725.

polgreen glamping

There's something about heading down an unmarked lane into a Cornish valley that just feels so right. Polgreen's particular unmarked lane slides almost unnoticed into the Vale of Mawgan, a few miles from the north coast. At the bottom, a sloping field sheltered by woodland and hidden by hedges is host to the satisfyingly retro sight of a scattering of cream-coloured bell tents.

Simon and Sarah, Polgreen's friendly owners, transform this little corner of their 40-acre farm into a glamping haven for just a short time over the school summer holidays every year. Six five and six-metre bell tents are positioned on their own little plots of levelled ground, with plenty of space around for those who enjoy a bit of privacy or yearn for a sylvan retreat. Each tent is furnished with a double bed, a double futon, an optional single mattress roll, a coffee table, a big hide rug and all the pots, pans, crockery, cutlery and so forth that usually reside in a kitchen. Further living space is provided by two communal dining tents, which are a big hit with families.

The facilities, all stationed just the other side of a bridge over a tiny brook, are designed to strike joy into the heart of the eco-conscious camper. Four compost loos are housed in delightful little sheds replete with antiquated reading matter, while two hot showers come complete with eco toiletries. There's a raised bed from which campers may harvest salad leaves, and pots of herbs with which they can garnish the cordon bleu dishes they've whipped up in the BBQ thoughtfully supplied with every pitch.

And there's really no excuse for not cooking up some mouth-watering food here. On site there is a small honesty shop selling freshly baked bread, local treats, breakfast and BBQ essentials. They also have a range of gastro glamping recipe cards, along with all the ingredients needed to make them. A ten-minute walk up a track leads to the Gluvian Farm Organics shop, where everything on sale has been produced on the owners' land (do ask for a taste of their yummy preserves). Barely any distance further, in the village of Trevarrian, you'll find equally appetising fare at the Bre-Pen Farm Shop. Meanwhile, down in Mawgan Porth, there's a former petrol station – now called Cornish Fresh – that looks like the sort of place that sells seaside holiday tat but that actually houses a deli with a wide range of ingredients destined to inspire all sorts of culinary greatness.

Polgreen is just a short hop from a clutch of Cornwall's best surfing beaches, as well as some of the most dramatic stretches of the South West Coast Path, so grab your wetsuit or boots and get out there. After a day on the beach, children can help feed Polgreen's ducks, fish, pigs and sheep, including the eminently strokeable pet ewe, Hettie. The kids can also keep a look out for the array of wildlife on the farm – from otters and roe deer to horseshoe bats, heron, snipe, and even the occasional bittern.

It's a bit of a shame that Cornwall Airport is just over the hill from Polgreen since it means that, when the wind is coming from the wrong direction, noise from planes and helicopters can impinge on the tranquillity of the site. However, most of the time all you'll hear is the wind in the trees, the calls of unseen wood pigeons and, if you listen carefully at night, the hoots and toowits of owls patrolling the dark woods.

St Mawgan, Cornwall (full address upon booking)
glampingcornwall.com

❊ There are 6 bell tents, each sleeping up to 5 guests. The site does allow campfires and each bell tent has its own fire brazier, BBQ and picnic bench outside. The Polgreen Pantry has free Wi-Fi access and this is where guests can also borrow beach gear, kid's bodyboards, board games and books. There's also 2 central dining shelters (with tables and chairs) and a honesty mini-bar cooler.

❊ The local area is renowned for its surf schools – try Kingsurf down at Mawgan Porth (01637 860091) – but you can also go sea fishing or diving (01637 850930). The sandy beach at Bedruthan Steps is amazing (though do check tide times first); Padstow and the Camel Trail are just 6 miles away.

❊ Polgreen has its own small honesty shop (the Polgreen Pantry) where you can pick up freshly baked bread, local treats, breakfast and BBQ essentials and gastro glamping recipe cards, along with all the ingredients to make them. Off site, take a stroll along a gated lane to manicured St Mawgan, home to the Falcon Inn (01637 860225) and its range of local ales. Watergate Bay is the home of Jamie Oliver's Cornish Fifteen (01637 861000) – very pricey but nicey. Right underneath is the less expensive but highly recommended Beach Hut (01637 860877). Farm shops worthy of a trip are Gluvian Farm Organics at Mawgan Porth (01637 860635) and Bre-Pen Farm Shop (01637 860420) in Trevarrian.

❊ The site is open only over the school summer holidays but offers bell tent hire for set up in other local locations out of season.

❊ Pre-booking is essential. Bell tents from £480 per week including the first 2 people and all the glamping extras. Additional adults at £18 per night; additional children 13 years and under £14 per night; babies and tots 2 years and under free.

yurts cornwall

Yurts Cornwall, Tremeer Farm, Lanteglos-by-Fowey, Cornwall PL23 1NN 01726 870545 yurtscornwall.com

✿ Four Mongolian-style yurts, each sleeping up to 5 people. There's a funky restored barn with modern kitchen facilities (including fridge and microwave), toilets and hot showers, plus table tennis, indoor badminton and volleyball. Gas and charcoal BBQs are also available for outside. Each yurt has its own firepit.

✿ You're very near Polkerris Beach, where you can enjoy sailing, wind-surfing, powerboating and more at the nearby Polkerris Beach Company (01726 813306). Otherwise grab your hiking boots and explore the nearby South West Coast Path. For a bit of Cornish culture, take a stroll down the narrow winding streets of Fowey Old Town, Polperro or Looe and browse the many individual galleries and shops.

✿ There are pork chops, sausages, bacon and eggs, apple juice and sometimes cider available from the farmhouse; and milk and bread can be pre-ordered from the milkman. If you fancy a night out with the kiddies, take them to Sam's (01726 832273), an American bistro in Fowey – they also have a place at Polkerris Beach (01726 812255).

✿ Open Easter–mid Oct.

✿ Mid July–end Aug the yurts are available for a full week only and are £795. Out of high season a week costs £495, and you can also arrange shorter mid-week breaks in April and May from £195.

Hidden away among a warren of high-banked, tree-lined Cornish lanes, Tremeer Farm is found. Its four, 18ft Mongolian-style yurts are well spaced, giving visitors plenty of room to roam, and all are comfortably furnished with wooden floors, cosy rugs, a wood-burning stove, plus a full-size bed with duvet. You can tell that owners Rob and Sara (both avid campers) have lavished lots of love and a good measure of hard work on the transformation of Tremeer from working farm to a beautiful glamping destination. But true to the farm's roots, you're bound to bump into one or two animals during your stay. In fact, you may find it hard to avoid pet Kune Kune pig Rosie, who just loves a belly rub – not to mention the clucking chickens, cute orphan lambs in the spring and the friendly Dexter cows in the field. Children can help with animal feeding in the mornings, allowing parents to chill out over a cup of coffee.

Cooking here can be a communal affair with the camp kitchens housed in a listed granary or 'The Big Barn'. Each kitchen is shared between two yurts and is well equipped with camp stove, fridge and everything you should need to prepare a hearty meal. Guests can also try their hand at producing pizza in the wood-fired pizza oven. The more adventurous can cook out on a BBQ or on a campfire under the stars. The set-up makes it a great place for groups too (up to 28 guests), who can hire all four yurts and the Long Barn – a large rustic playbarn, full of character and perfect to congregate in if the weather turns British.

As for things to do, you'll be spoilt for choice. The site is only a short distance from Fowey, one of Cornwall's most popular seaside towns, and is surrounded by stunning walking routes (the South West Coast Path is just over a mile away). When you're done, soak your tired muscles in the wood-fired hot tub back at camp, before melting marshmallows under the stars – glamping the Cornish way!

botelet farm

Botelet Farm, Herodsfoot, Liskeard, Cornwall PL14 4RD 01503 220225 botelet.com

❀ The numbers at Botelet Farm are limited partly by the facilities. There's a single hot shower (with piped Radio 3 so you can sing along in the morning) and a single toilet. Cold taps are dotted around and there's a trough for washing dishes. Campfires are permitted in the pits provided and the yurts have wood-burning stoves. Recently the site has also introduced excellent in-house therapy treatments. Campers can enjoy a massage in a treatment space that may be a room inside one of the historic cottages or the yurts, or try an al fresco massage in a quiet corner of the farm when the weather is fair!

Visitors are advised to book in advance. See the website for full details.
❀ Try the Polmartin Riding School (01503 220428) just down the road, which offers lessons for all ages and abilities. Prices start at £25 for a group lesson or ride.
❀ The farm sells eggs when available and does a veggie breakfast in the farmhouse at £15 per person (book the night before). Otherwise there's a Spar in Pelynt, about 4 miles away. The nearest pub (4 miles away) is The Plough (01503 262556) in Duloe, which has a warm, inviting atmosphere and great local food.
❀ Open Easter–mid Sept for the yurts/end Sept for tents.
❀ £7.50 per person, per night, for tents. The yurts (sleeping 2) are £180 for 2 nights/£380 for a week.

Botelet Farm is almost like a separate small village: it has its own phone box and genuine Victorian red postbox, and room for just a couple of tents and a few extra guests. Actually there's space for hundreds of tents in Botelet's 300 acres, but it's a working farm and the owners want to keep it small and special. The two tent pitches change with the season, based on where the cows are grazing, how high the grass is, and a number of other factors. All of which means that if you come here every year for the rest of your camping days the chances are you'd never pitch in the same place twice.

In addition to these ever-changing pitches, Botelet Farm is also home to a pair of magnificent yurts, one in the field out front and the other in a separate meadow above the farm. More unfazed by the movements of the cattle and the migration of the birds, these structures reside in their spots all season, both with excellent views across the rolling valley beyond. Inside, the furnishings are simple and rustic but more than adequate, while both have wood-burning stoves in their centres, to warm those chilly nights and boil the kettle for your morning cuppa.

Keeping to the agricultural feel, features around Botelet have been ingeniously converted to give a camping practicality to the working farm. A cattle trough has been altered to work as a large, long sink for washing-up and, inside one of the old farm cottages, a space has been created for owner Tia to offer therapeutic massage treatments. Not that it's her go-to spot. When the weather permits, the massage couch, with heated under-blanket, is taken outside for al fresco massages in the sun and sometimes even inside the yurts themselves.

Off site, trails lead around the perimeter of the fields and into the adjacent woodland, while a 10-minute walk takes you to Bury Down Hill Fort, a Neolithic structure with panoramic views across the Cornish countryside. Beneath, the farm meadows spread, peppered by cows grazing and no doubt wondering where they'll be moving to next. Masters of the meadows, it's still they who call the shots.

the lake

Naming your new glampsite should be simple, right? Most owners highlight the one stand-out feature which sets the place apart. Easy. Unfortunately for Rupert and Fran – owners of Cornwall's newest glamping venture – they've created a getaway with half a dozen headliners. Take the location: hidden by a disused china clay quarry, worked from the Victorian era until the 1940s, the site provides exploring opportunities a-plenty for history buffs. Then there's the accommodation itself: a converted shipping container from China, which once roamed foreign seas. Or how about the wildlife? From grazing Galloway cattle to migrating Canadian geese and swooping sand martins. However, in the end, Rupert and Fran opted simply for The Lake – "having your very own spring-fed lake in which to swim, row a boat or cast a line feels like the icing on the cake". We think they picked wisely.

After a couple of wrong turns and some unexpected off-roading, guests arrive by car, which is swiftly abandoned – often for the entirety of their stay – before being warmly greeted for check-in. But this is no ordinary check-in: opening the industrial container lock-by-lock feels like unwrapping a giant Christmas present, quickly morphing into a cosy cabin. Inside, the design is simple, functional and contemporary – probably owing to Rupert's Scandinavian roots – and comes with a comfortable double bed, fully equipped kitchen, double-glazed French windows, LED lighting throughout and warmth supplied by a small wood-burning stove. The ablution facilities, all stationed at the rear of the container, are designed to strike joy into the heart of the eco-conscious glamper. The hot showers – and we mean hot – are solar-powered (the site is completely off-grid), and the water is pumped directly from the lake. Sorry, we mean *your* lake.

Any negatives? Well, the surrounding area comes under 'Countryside Rights of Way Act 2000', meaning you may see a dog walker or the odd soldier scurrying through. Yes, you read that correctly. Survival courses – often the last exercise before being deployed to war

– occasionally take place on Bodmin Moor's stark expanse, sometimes involving Chinook helicopters and mock battles! This is, of course, not everyone's idea of serenity, but for most makes incredible viewing.

As for things to do in the area, when we asked Rupert for suggestions, he replied, "Why would you want to leave?" And after spending a couple of hours exploring the crumbling Victorian ruins and watching in awe as moorland ponies clip-clop to the water's edge for an evening drink, we couldn't help but agree. What you do here is up to you; drift away on the boat like Huckleberry Finn, build an evening fire or climb the short, but extremely fun, white sand mountain and make friends with the resident raven, who sits atop surveying the tranquil jade water below. Difficult decisions indeed. But not nearly as hard as naming your cool new glampsite.

The Lake, Glynn Valley, China Clay Works, Maidenwell, Cardinham, Bodmin, Cornwall PL30 4DW
01579 321263

❉ The container features a comfortable double bed, duvet, pillows, blankets, storage space, table and chairs, LED lighting throughout, 2 USB phone/iPad charging points, books, torch, fishing rod, wood-burning stove and a portable BBQ. The kitchen has hot and cold running water on demand, a 3-ring gas hob and oven, sink, kettle, and plenty of cutlery and crockery. The accommodation is off-grid (powered by solar panels), with 1 hot shower and 1 toilet attached to the back of the container. Eco-friendly shampoo and shower gel are also provided. The 80ft-deep lake is lovely to swim in and a small rowing boat can be provided for £20/day. Please do note, though, that swimming and boating are done at your own risk.
❉ There are stacks of things to do locally if the mood takes you – from exploring the 17,000+ unspoiled acres of Bodmin Moor, with its treeless heaths and bogs, to visiting historic Restormel Castle (03703 331181) for a picnic with 360-degree views of the Cornish countryside and the River Fowey. For something a little more adventurous, head to Adrenalin Quarry (01579 308204) and soar 50m above a flooded quarry at heart-pumping speeds, or walk the South West Coast Path to enjoy some of the most spectacular sections of the English coastline.
❉ A welcome pack of essentials is provided on arrival, but please remember that the site is extremely remote and the nearest shop is 8 miles away so you might want to bring your own supplies or use Rupert and Fran's food service, where shopping can be pre-ordered to be waiting for you on arrival. There is no fridge, but a cage (which hangs off the jetty) keeps milk, margarine and beers cool. Local pubs – relatively speaking – include the cosy St Tudy Inn (01208 850656), the London Inn (01579 326756) and the Blisland Inn (01208 850739), the winner of CAMRA's National Pub of the Year in 2001.
❉ Open all year.
❉ Low season: £100 per night (minimum 2 nights), 7 nights £550. High season: £125 per night (minimum 2 nights), 7 nights £700.

koa tree camp

"What's a Koa Tree", you ask? Well, in Hawaiian culture, the resourceful Koa Tree was used to whittle the hardy canoes and longboards used to ride the choppy Pacific waves. While the North Devon coast might be a few thousand miles (geographically, at least) from paradisical south sea islands, the 'Aloha Spirit' is well and truly alive at this glamp-tastic south-west site. The brainchild of lifelong pals Andy and Sam, Koa Tree Camp encapsulates those twin totems of Hawaiian culture – nature and surfing. Who says luxury camping has to just mean lazing about in your fancy yurt, cabin or bell tent all weekend? Sure, the spacious digs, fully equipped 'surf-shack' kitchen facilities, private underfloor-heated bathrooms and snug rainy-day room call out to the inner loafer. But at Koa Tree Camp, there's also a jam-packed schedule of activities and events to suit everyone, from cookery courses to outdoor cinema evenings, pizza nights to performances by local musicians. Naturally, of course, there's also an onsite surf school, which is perfect for the novice and the beach bunny alike. Be sure to check the calendar a few weeks before you arrive to find out what's on during your stay.

Despite all this luxury, Sam and Andy won't compromise on their green credentials – water is recycled and renewable heating and wood-burning stoves are used throughout. The boys' philosophy even extends to the wonderful onsite community shop, which is positively blooming with organic fruit and veg from their very own market garden and orchard. For a true taste of life on a working farm, why not help out with the livestock and learn about permaculture from the farmers themselves? Guests can even enjoy a spot of *boules* or get a game of headers 'n' volleys going on the mini football pitch. After all that exertion, while away your evenings round the communal firepit or supping scrumpy at sunset by the tranquil farmyard pond.

Koa Tree Camp, Hollacombe Farm, Welcombe, Bideford, Devon EX39 6HE 07492 750861 koatreecamp.com

❀ Five yurts (sleeping 6), 3 log cabins (sleeping 4) and 2 bell tents (sleeping 3). Electricity is provided to all of the yurts. Each yurt and bell tent has its own BBQ and cooking equipment. A newly converted facilities barn provides a communal kitchen and rainy day room equipped with ping-pong table, comfy sitting room with board games and books, and a Wi-Fi connection. There are 6 private bathrooms with bath/shower, WC and sink. Underfloor heating runs throughout the barn and there's also a large wood-burning stove. The hot water is run on renewable energy and recycled using grey-water recycling systems. Campfires allowed in the communal firepit.

❀ The site is ideally situated to explore both the North Devon and Cornish coastlines. The South West Coast Path takes in some of the area's most stunning stretches, including Welcombe Mouth, Clovelly, Hartland Quay and Lighthouse, and the picturesque fishing village of Boscastle – thankfully on the mend after the disastrous floods of 2004. Koa Tree Camp can arrange several aqua-tivities, including coasteering and surfing (see the website for board- and wetsuit-hire fees).

❀ The onsite Welcombe Community Shop is volunteer run and opens all year round. It stocks a wide range of fairtrade basics and groceries, including organic seasonal fruit and veg from the onsite market garden and orchard. The Old Smithy Inn (01288 331305) is just a short drive from the site and serves up some lovely pub grub and even lovelier ales and ciders – all under a 13th-century thatched roof. For a wider selection of restaurants and pubs, jump in the car and head to Bude (around 11 miles away).

❀ Open April–Nov.

❀ Bookings accepted for short breaks (Mon–Fri; Fri–Mon) and for full weeks (Fri–Fri). Low season: Yurts £330 (short break) £640 (week); bells £240 (short break) £460 (week); wood-burning stove cabins £310 (short break) £590 (week). High season: Yurts £400 (short break) £750 (week); bells £310 (short break) £580 (week); wood-burning stove cabins £360 (short break) £680 (week). Greater flexibility is provided for large groups.

loveland farm

Having toured the world as hotshot designer duo 'Griffin', fashionistas Jeff and Karina decided to trade in the glamourous world of haute couture for the simple pleasures of rural Devon. And what a spot they found. Nestled between the lush undulating hills and wild North Devon coast, Loveland Farm is six acres of pastoral paradise. The small holding's 19th-century farmhouse and ancient out-buildings are today home to your wonderfully accommodating hosts and their design studio.

In keeping with tradition, the Griffins have a veritable menagerie of animals on site, including Oxford Sandy Black pigs, chickens, lambs and even a pair of Asian water buffaloes, who spend their days beautifying in the stream at the bottom of the field.

Accommodation-wise, guests are spoiled for choice. Loveland's wholly inclusive ethos means there are six pitches set aside for tents, campervans and caravans, but it's the five uniquely designed pods that really catch your attention. The Popla Pod sleeps two adults and is perfect for those wanting their own exclusive getaway; the Welcombe Pod sleeps up to four in a bright and spacious dome; and the mammoth twin Eden and Hartland Pods sleep six apiece – each contains a gorgeous handmade tipi inside creating an clever, internal double bedroom. The catwalk queen here, though, is undoubtedly the Loveland Pod. Bright, modern and über-luxurious, this geodesic glamping dome sits atop pristine raised decking with expansive views of the woodland meadow below and the sea beyond. Fitted with a designer's eye for detail, the pod comes with a king-sized bed and two spacious sofa beds, comfortably sleeping six. You'll find a wood-burning stove for extra cosiness, plus a host of other mod cons. There's even a projector for your own private movie nights! Each pod also has its own separate cabin where guests have a private a loo, shower and fully equipped kitchenette.

Loveland Farm isn't purely about the sartorial, though – there's substance behind the style. Jeff and Karina are passionate about sustainability. The entire complex is run off of solar panels, while vibrant pastel beach huts house eco-showers and compost loos for the tent campers. They grow their own veg and even get milk from the aforementioned water buffaloes. Self-sufficiency indeed.

If you can drag yourself away from the farm, the local area is brimming with great day trips. The Hartland Peninsula has a stunning array of unique flora, fauna and marine life, and the historic fishing village of Clovelly is also worth a trip – grab some fresh seafood to accompany the farm's own homegrown treats.

Loveland Farm, Hartland, Devon EX39 6AT
01237 441894 lovelandfarmcamping.co.uk

❉ Five uniquely designed pods sleeping 2–6 and 6 spacious camping pitches. Pods come fully furnished and accompanied by a private kitchen cabin, toilet and shower room. Campers have access to 3 composting loos set up on site inside the beach huts (one is specially designed for children) and a hot solar-powered shower. A communal washing-up area sits next to the beach huts. Designated firepits, BBQ and drinking water point.

❉ The surf in North Devon is great, with popular beaches such as Bude, Westward Ho!, Saunton Sands, and Croyde and Woolacombe just up the coast. There are loads of great surf schools in the area: check out Big Blue Surf School (01288 331764) in Bude for a session with Jon Price, coach to the British surfing team. If you just want to get out there, visit eyeballhq.tv for live webcams, tide times and daily weather conditions for the entire North Devon Coast. The Tarka Trail runs for 180 miles from Barnstaple to Bideford. While you can walk the route you can also cycle along the trail which is also connects to the National Cycle Network's Devon coast-to-coast path to Plymouth. You could also explore Lundy Island, just

offshore, which is managed by the Landmark Trust and accessible by boat from Clovelly (Clovelly Charters 01237 431405) and Bideford (MS Oldenburg 01271 863636). There are also helicopter flights during the winter months. Boats leave daily and cost around £35 for a day return; admission to the island costs £5.

❉ You'll find no fresher produce than the farm's own fresh eggs, outdoor reared Loveland pork sausages and ham/bacon joints. The Hart Inn (01237 441474) is a wonderful independent pub in the heart of the village serving great local ales and an exceptional and eclectic menu using locally sourced ingredients, as well as a classic bar menu. The afternoon Sunday roasts are a popular local favourite, so be sure to book at the weekends. The Old Smithy Inn (01288 331305) in Welcombe is a traditional friendly freehouse serving hearty pub grub and real ales. It's also the place to hear live music – on the Tuesday night Jam Night or the monthly folk club.

❉ Pods open all year; camping mid March–end of Oct.

❉ Camping pitches between £15–£20 (depending on season). Kids are £8–£10 (depending on season); Pod prices vary: 3 night stay £285–£470; 4 night stay £340–£600; Full week £595–£1,050.

longlands

Armed with little more than a collection of *Cool Camping* guidebooks and their cherished 1965 Splittie, Bella, Bugsie and the kids hit the open road in 2010 with a view to permanently escaping the hustle and bustle of London. Over the course of three years the family travelled up to the Outer Hebrides (twice!), down to Devon, took weekend trips to the New Forest and enjoyed a wonderful summer travelling through France, all the while making notes describing what made each site special and contemplating the idea of opening their very own glamping getaway.

When the family decided to leave London they were looking for a location with some very specific requirements: conveniently close to the sea (to be able to sneak in a lunchtime surf!), breathtaking views and plenty of space to create the ultimate rural retreat. Months passed before Bella and Bugsie set eyes on a delightful destination on the western border of Exmoor, only five minutes from the picturesque coastal village of Combe Martin. In July 2012, that destination became Longlands – and we think you'll love it...

The accommodation at Longlands is as picturesque as its natural surroundings, with five thoughtfully positioned, identical safari tents (sleeping six) furnished with vintage leather sofas, luxurious linen and a blanket box filled with family-friendly games.

At the heart of each lodge is a fully equipped kitchen with a wood-burning stove, keeping the cosy interior warm in all weathers while also providing a means of cooking. Not finished there, each country-inspired abode has its very own shower room and separate en suite bathroom, with flushing loo and basin, plus a wide range of natural aromatherapy products.

After you've spent a memorable day exploring North Devon and its many delights, Longlands is a comforting enclave to return to each night. Bella and Bugsie have done their hosting homework, pre-empting every need. The 'Longlands Larder' is testimony to that, with hard-to-resist, local produce (milk, jam, chutney and cheese) stocked 24 hours a day. Guests can also cook on their private BBQ, overlooking the sheltered valley and rolling hills all the way to the sea. Allow your days to float by effortlessly, while enjoying the simplicity of field living – albeit in a luxury canvas lodge.

**Longlands Farm, Coulsworthy, Combe Martin,
North Devon EX34 0PD 01271 882004
longlandsdevon.co.uk**

❀ Five fully equipped luxury safari lodges (each sleeping 6) housing a king bedroom, twin bedroom and a double cabin bed. There's a wood-burning stove (can also be used for cooking – either on top, as you would on a hob, or in its oven compartment), small gas ring, sink, cooking utensils, pots, pans, crockery, cutlery and everything you could need, including fresh herbs and condiments. Three-seater leather vintage Chesterfield and blanket box, filled with games. Each lodge has its own en suite shower room (and separate washroom), with proper flushing loo. Hot water for the shower, sink and basin is provided by a wood-burning boiler. All bed and bath linens are provided, plus a range of natural aromatherapy bathroom products. Large deck area at the front of the lodge with sofa, table and chairs with fabulous views over the lake and valley, private BBQ area with fire bowl and a bench. Charcoal and marshmallows are available from the larder shop and BBQ baskets can be ordered from the menu.

❀ Meet the real 'Beast of Exmoor' – be a keeper for the day, or feed the lemurs, meerkats and penguins at Exmoor Zoo (01598 763352). Discover a house full of treasures and secrets, spy on rare horseshoe bats and enjoy a carriage ride at nearby Arlington Court (01271 850296). The Wildlife and Dinosaur Park in Combe Martin (01271 882486) is only 2 miles from Longlands: visitors can swim with sea lions, feed the lions, shadow a keeper, or fly a bird of prey (not literally of course!). Take a short trip (5 miles) to Watermouth Castle Theme Park (01271 867474) and descend into the dungeons, get lost in a maze and marvel at the Watershow Extravaganza. Finally, all you budding artists can indulge your creative side at Paint a Pot Studios in Braunton (01271 813999). Take some time out to create a ceramic masterpiece; they will even post your creation home to you once it has been glazed and fired.

❀ The 'Longlands Larder' is a 24-hour onsite shop. It has all the essentials such as butter, milk, jam, chutney and cheese, and many not-so-essentials (crisps, nuts, olives and chocolates). Longlands can also cater for every meal of your stay, should you wish to try their freshly baked bread pastries, pies, pasties, suppers and desserts. The site also has a licence and can provide local ciders, beers and wines.

❀ The Fox & Goose in Parracombe (01598 763239) is the nearest pub to Longlands (4 miles). It serves great food, has a wonderful atmosphere and is a favourite with locals. The Black Venus (01598 763251) in Challacombe is highly recommended – around 6 miles from the site – or, for something a bit different, head over to Ilfracombe to the restaurant of artist Damien Hirst at The Quay (01271 868090). His gallery, Other Criteria, is also on the quayside right next door to the restaurant.

❀ Open mid March–early Nov

❀ Midweek breaks (Monday to Friday) start at £575; weekends (Friday to Monday) start at £595.

the orchard retreat

The Orchard Retreat, East Forde Farm, Cheriton Fitzpaine, Crediton EX17 4BA 01363 866058 theorchardretreat.co.uk

✤ Three yurts with a private bathroom for each and a communal kitchen near a large lawn for outdoor games. There's also 'The Gallery' with Wi-Fi, games and books, loo, washing machine and tumble dryer. A small onsite shop offers locally sourced items, and a mobile masseuse can be arranged, giving massages within your yurt.
✤ Stroll along the river banks at Bickleigh (6 miles away) before dropping by the Devon Railway Centre (01884 855671) and Bickleigh Mill (01884 855419); the former boasts a restaurant and a small selection of shops. Yearlstone Vineyard (01884 855700), situated on a

hillside just above the river Exe, offers wine tours as well as a café and shop. A little further on from Yearlstone lies Knightshayes (01884 254665), a lovely country house with extensive grounds and a walled kitchen garden, along with a wonderful café housed in the old stable block.
✤ Thornes Farm Shop (01363 866541) is next to the site, where you can pick your own fruit, buy local meats for the BBQ or have coffee and homemade cake in the café. Pub-wise, you can walk the 20 minutes to the Ring of Bells (01363 860111) in the village. The owners are passionate about cooking local, seasonal produce as well as stocking regional beer and cider.
✤ Yurt season March–Oct; the Cider Barn and Apple Tree Cottage available all year round.
✤ From £275 for a 3–4 night stay during low season.

There's a good chance once you've found this farmland glamping site, that you'll never want to leave. Nestled among some of the most glorious countryside in south-west England, The Orchard Retreat offers three locally handcrafted yurts – Bramley, Pippin and Russet (named after the surrounding apple trees) – each dotted on a sloping four-acre orchard, surrounded by fields and streams, all within the site. So why not swing over to Devon to take a detox from the digital world?

Each dwelling comes furnished in a stylish and romantic way – from the stable doors, comprised of a mixture of ash, chestnut and hazel, to the wood-burning stove and warm rugs, guests can envelop themselves in a truly luxurious camping experience. This family-run business is clearly a labour of love for owners Nick and Vicky, who understand that creating a memorable glampsite takes more than just plonking some yurts in a field and leaving you to it. The 'Facilities Lodge' is testament to that. Follow the path lit by solar lanterns and you will find a private bathroom complete with shower, sink and flushing loo. There's a shared kitchen for cooking, too, plus a firepit and communal cob pizza oven, though many take advantage of their own private BBQ and picnic table.

As for offsite activities, thankfully nature has laid on a smorgasbord of adventures to savour. Bring a bike and explore the tranquil Grand Western Canal Cycle Route, which runs through the heart of Devon. Often along the towpath this flat and mainly off-road route is ideal for families with children, offering sweeping landscape views, varying between sheltered woodlands and the lofty plateaus of the Blackdown Hills. But it's not all about the great outdoors; the lively market town of Crediton, just a 15-minute drive away, is best known for St Boniface Church and boasts one of the country's best farmers' markets, while it is around 20 minutes to the city of Exeter, home to a magnificent gothic cathedral with a perfect apron of grass out front for enjoying picnics in the sun.

Whether you want to wander through enchanted woods, play in streams, or simply escape the hustle and bustle of everyday life, you can revel at this sizeable slice of glamping perfection. "Off-grid living at its very best" is how Nick and Vicky describe a stay at The Orchard Retreat. And as you unwind outside your secluded, homely yurt, tucking into tasty local produce and savouring those delightful countryside views, you can't help but think that's a fair assessment.

huntstile organic farm

Huntstile is foodie heaven. Owners Lizzie and John radiate a passion for good food, as does their farm, which covers over 650 acres of organic land, nursing vegetables, soft fruit, wheat, oats and barley, as well as sheep, pigs, goats, cows and chickens galore. This isn't a dedicated campsite but a farm-cum-campsite/glamping-sort-of-a-place – and it's amazing. You can even get married here.

On the site there are 25 pitches for campers, which are located in a separate field just down from the farmhouse. But, if that seems too much like hard work, then you can just cosy up in the beautiful bowtop gypsy caravan – complete with dinky little wood-burning stove and double bed – or in a gorgeous, sky-blue shepherd's hut trailer which, believe it or not, sleeps four, albeit at a bit of a squeeze. Both have an outdoor firepit and a BBQ for cooking.

You're in Quantock country, so the farm lies in an enviable position, circled by stunning rural Somerset and all its outdoor possibilities, not to mention a lovely stretch of coastline within walking distance. There are also onsite walks that seek out ancient woodland or stone circles – it's hard to believe you're only 10 minutes from the M5! Just a short stroll across the farmyard is a gorgeous little café, where you can tuck into a cream tea or a Full English, happy in the knowledge that it's all fair trade without a GM ingredient in sight. Lizzie also runs sausage-making courses, so you can have fun creating, and then sampling, your very own British bangers.

Huntstile Organic Farm, Goathurst, Nr Bridgwater, Somerset TA5 2DQ 01278 662358
huntstileorganicfarm.co.uk

❀ One gypsy caravan (sleeping 2), 1 shepherd's hut (sleeping 2 adults and 2 small children) and 25 regular camping pitches (2 with electric hook-ups). There are 2 electric showers next to the main toilets and washing-up area, and a composting loo in the camping field.

❀ The beautiful Quantock Hills are within a 5-mile drive and offer a range of outdoor activities, including walking, horseriding, climbing and fishing. The fossils and freshwater ponds of Kilve Beach, on the north Somerset coast, are only a 20 minutes' drive away.

❀ Onsite organic café and veg garden. Breakfast available every day; supper by request. Yummy basics may also be bought on site when available. Elsewhere, chomp on juicy burgers at the Pines Restaurant Diner (01823 451245) in Broomfield, 3 miles south, or homemade venison and Stilton pies at the Lamb Inn (01278 671350), 4 miles north in Spaxton.

❀ Open April–Oct.

❀ Gypsy caravan £60, shepherd's hut £75 (both 2-night minimum stay; breakfast included).

dimpsey glamping

It was around the time Em and Andrew were thinking about a shepherd's hut that Em began to consider designing and selling interior accessories. It's now easy to see why. "The hut is like a five-star hotel in a field", she explains as we swing open the grey-blue, two-part door. Inside, the eye for detail is incredible, with not only every item you could possibly need but also artwork on the walls, rustic bronze fittings, candles, ornaments and a stash of comfortable pillows. There's a wealth of goodies waiting in store but everything has its place – even the steaming welcome tea tray that's there on your arrival!

Perhaps we gush a bit. After all, this is hardly humble shepherd's camping, what with an en suite shower room, but there's still a very tangible element of the outdoors here. Outside, a BBQ and firepit are accompanied by a hanging grill, and you can grab the telescope under your bed to make the most of the night skies.

"We wanted something that would suit the style of our 500-year-old farm", Em goes on, gesturing towards the animals and describing the "mosaic of countryside". There's something fitting about the shepherd's hut within the rolls of open landscape and, as if to accentuate this appropriateness, there's a second hut on site – the very one featured in the 2015 film version of *Far From The Madding Crowd*, with the exact interiors used in the film and Carey Mulligan's signature on the wall! For an extra price, the hut can be set up as a private cinema – the perfect treat after steaming in the site's wood-fired hot tub.

The Blackdown Hills have been a designated Area of Outstanding Natural Beauty since 1991 and here on Beetham Farm, Dimpsey Glamping manages to match it all for beauty. The interior of the hut, like something out of *Country Living*, emulates the beauty on the doorstep, and the traditional types of activities that are best enjoyed here like walking, cycling or horseriding. It's also an easy journey down to the Jurassic Coast, half an hour away – and there's a flask in the hut so you can take a cuppa with you.

It all fits like hand in glove – a place that shepherds of old could probably only dream of. Just inside the hut there is a quaint ode to all their hard work – a tiny postcard painting of a shepherd in the field, leaning peacefully against his crook. Small, unnoticeable yet wonderfully well placed, it's just another little feature that shows the thought that's been put into this magical place.

Dimpsey Glamping, Beetham Farm, Beetham, Combe St Nicholas, Chard, Somerset TA20 3PY
01460 477770 dimpsey.co.uk

❋ The 18ft-long shepherd's hut features full en suite facilities, including shower, flushing loo and bathroom products. The hut is sheep's wool-insulated and has a wood-burning stove with a free, unlimited supply of wood. The double bed (linen and bedding provided) can be folded into the wall if more space is required. There is a long sofa, a practical area with gas hob, fridge, sink and all the utensils and cutlery you'll need, plus a hand-built oak table and benches for 4–6 people. Games, books, a radio, telescope, OS maps and star maps are all there, too. Outside there's a BBQ and campfire area, a wood-fired pizza oven and a hot tub, plus the second hut from the *Far From the Madding Crowd* movie.

❋ Dimpsey is a small, mixed farm with 15 Dexter cows, 10 Jacobs sheep and 2 Tamworth pigs; 15 acres are a designated SSSI, so expect plenty of varied wildlife, too.

❋ Walking and cycling routes surround the campsite, and other activities (horseriding, clay pigeon shooting, fishing trips and more) can be arranged on request. There are tourist leaflets and an OS map of the local area. If you want to stretch your legs further, driving the 35 minutes to the coast is always a safe bet. Walk the beaches of Lyme Regis, Charmouth fossil beach or Burton Bradstock. The National Trust properties of Barrington Court (01460 242614) – a 16th-century Tudor Mansion – and the exceptional gardens of Montacute House (01935 823289), are both well worth a visit.

❋ Subject to availability you can buy a selection of food directly from the farm, including burgers made from their own Dexter beef, sausages from their pigs, lamb burgers and, of course, farm-fresh eggs. Just ask what's available during your stay – or pre-order by email.

❋ Nearby places to eat include the gastro-style Candlelight Inn (01460 234476), 1 mile away, and Hugh Fearnley-Whittingstall's River Cottage Canteen (01297 630314), in Axminster.

❋ Open all year.

❋ £125 per night for 2 people (price including bacon, eggs, milk, bread and butter for your first breakfast).

crafty camping

For anyone who has dreamed of finding that secluded, sylvan sanctuary, look no further than Crafty Camping. The brainchild of expert woodsman Guy Mallinson (of BBC's *Mastercrafts* fame), this entirely hand-crafted glamping Shangri-La sits snugly carved into several acres of West Dorset woodland.

Originally the base for Guy's woodcraft workshops, this herbaceous hideaway was born out of his pupils' pleadings for camping in the forest. Thanks to the persistence of these novice whittlers, this tranquil woodland paradise is now welcoming peace-and-quiet-loving adults for genuine fuss-free glamping, all year round.

Nestled amid this dreamy landscape are Guy's labours of love: a tipi, two yurts, three bell tents and a shepherd's hut. Adorned with reindeer skins and containing king-sized beds with oak bedsteads (hand-carved, of course), hammocks and all the other bits and bobs you're likely to need, these luxurious lodgings each have their own private decking area. All (except the bell tents) have a private proper flushing loo as well as a private 'tree shower' beneath the forest canopy. The three bell tents share the woven willow shower and grass-topped his 'n' hers, proper plumbed loos.

The safari-style, *Out of Africa* field kitchen surpasses those in most apartments, with a good gas range, counters and decent utensils, cutlery and crockery. The wood-fired pizza oven just shouts rustic charm – and there's nothing like pulling out a gooey, lightly charred margherita pizza to tear and share under the bivouac.

Space and seclusion are the common themes here. Wherever you stay, you'll be amazed at the serenity and stillness of the place. No man is an island, though, and for those of a social nature, Guy has conscientiously kitted out a communal yurt with comfy couches, a library and board games.

Guy likens it to "Avatar in summer and Narnia in winter" – a pretty apt description. We'll plump for a cross between Tolkien and *A Midsummer Night's Dream*. With a woodland inhabited by buzzards, foxes, deer and badgers, not to mention a small fishing pond teeming with rainbow trout, it's positively Edenesque. It will come as no surprise that there have been more than a few marriage proposals here. This is a real romantic retreat. Oh, and did we mention the sauna yurt?

The level of care, skill and attention to detail is astounding. The yurts (some of the finest we've ever seen) are made from the woodland's own coppiced chestnut, worked with nothing more than axes, drawknives and steam bending. "Everything is designed to return to nature without a trace if we were ever to leave the woods" says Guy – though something tells us he won't be leaving this woodland anytime soon.

**Crafty Camping, Mallinson Ltd, Woodland Workshop,
Yonder Hill, Holditch, West Dorset TA20 4NL
01460 221102 mallinson.co.uk**

❉ Yurt, tipi and shepherd's hut all with their own private,
flushing loo and private 'tree shower'. Three bells tents
share the woven willow shower and grass-topped his 'n'
hers proper flushing loo. There's a communal yurt with
craft library, board games, a small shop and information/
maps. The field kitchen has a wood-fired pizza oven and
full catering facilities. Each tent also has its own private
deck with BBQ, hammock, chairs and table and kelly
kettle. There is a sauna yurt and trout fishing pond.
Optional woodcraft courses are available on site.

❉ West Dorset has no end of charming coastal towns and
stunning beaches, including Chesil and West Bay. It's also
Thomas Hardy country and there are plenty of spots on
the Hardy trail for literary pilgrims, most notably the
Hardy Monument (01297 489481) and Thomas Hardy's
Cottage (01305 262366). The epic Jurassic Coast
(a UNESCO World Heritage Site) is just 12 miles away. For
walks, the views from Golden Cap (Dorset's highest cliff)
take some beating.

❉ Complimentary Dorset Cereals and tea and coffee
are available to all glamping guests. For the finest local
produce, head to Millers Farm Shop (01297 35290) in
Axeminster – it also stocks cider from Lyme Bay Winery
and Perry's Cider Mill. Bridport Market is the place to go
for a bargain, with a farmers' market on the second
Saturday of each month. The Tytherleigh Arms (01460
220214) is a cracking little 16th-century coaching inn,
just a short stroll from the site. It has a great menu
of reasonably priced Dorset fare and local ales from
the award-winning Otter and Branscombe breweries.

❉ Open all year.

❉ Bell tents from £88 per night; yurts, tipi and shepherd's
hut from £126 per night; 2 nights' minimum weekdays,
3 nights' minimum weekends.

old bidlake farm

Old Bidlake Farm, Broadoak, Bridport, Dorset DT6 5PY
01308 538080 oldbidlake-farm-camping.co.uk

❀ Four fully equipped bell tents, each furnished with beds for up to 2 adults or a family of 5, and a couple of retro caravans. Some bedding is provided but campers should bring their own sleeping bags or duvets. Cutlery, crockery and cookware are also provided, along with lanterns, a water carrier and a family-size freezer box. Outside your tent you'll find a wood-burning stove and a picnic table for dining al fresco. In the nearby barn are 2 private washrooms complete with flush toilets, hand basins and electric showers. Next door the camp kitchen features camping cookers, an electric oven, a fridge and freezer, a dining area and a sink. The small honesty shop in 'The Potting Shed' provides fresh eggs and seasonal fruit and veg, plus other basics. The small scale of the site makes it ideal for small groups looking to hire the whole site.

❀ The charming market town of Bridport is just 2 miles away, with a varied selection of independent shops to please foodies, book worms and art-lovers alike. The market on Wednesdays and Saturdays is a delight – check out the quirky mix of stalls selling everything from pots of homemade curry to antiques, bric-a-brac and crafts.
❀ The Ilchester Arms (01308 422600) at Symonsbury is a child-friendly, 15th-century village pub with an open fireplace, serving good food and local ales. Half a mile away, Washingpool Farm Shop (01308 459549) sells a wide selection of produce from local farms and bakeries, while Samways Fishmongers in West Bay (01308 422201) is the place to get your fresh seafood.
❀ Open April–Sept.
❀ Bell tents Fri–Sun £200–£300; Mon–Fri £200–£300; full week £325–£525. Retro Caravans from £40 per night; Bring your own Bell pitches with access to the glamping facilities from £24 per couple per night.

Cradled between the beautiful beaches of the Jurassic Coast and Dorset's highest hills lies the Marshwood Vale, home to a stunningly picturesque landscape, which is little changed since the area provided the backdrop to some of Thomas Hardy's best-known novels. However, the comfort and convenience of Old Bidlake Farm's camping field, with its four ready-erected bell tents, is most certainly up-to-date.

Making your arrival up the well-trodden track, you park in the farmyard where the wonderfully welcoming Sue will meet you with a tin of her delicious homemade apple cakes and show you around the eight acres of quiet pastureland. Guiding you through the pretty orchard, which at night is illuminated by a row of appealing solar lights, you're taken to the secluded meadow field. Nestled within each outward corner of the camping area are four traditional canvas bell tents. Each is named after the four hills that surround the field, and is equipped with a double futon and up to three child-sized futons, solar-powered lanterns, hot-water bottles, crockery and a cool-box – and there's also a toilet in the wooden wash hut if you don't fancy walking to the shower block in the barn extension at night. They also have a retro caravan if you don't want to sleep under canvas.

Outside, you'll find a picnic table and tree stumps fashioned into chairs to sit on while you cook under the stars on the very efficient rocket stoves. For more ambitious meals, the cosy field shelter houses a gas camping stove, portable wood-fired pizza oven and stove-top smoker, and the nearby barn kitchen has an oven, microwave, fridge and freezer, running hot water and a large dining table where you can enjoy communal meals.

Kids will feel like the Famous Five as they ride their bikes, fly kites and help out collecting eggs or picking the fruit and veg. They can even go riding at the stables next door – and, if they tire of that, the dramatic Jurassic Coast beach at Eype is only three miles away, with the lively fishing harbour of West Bay just a 15-minute drive.

honeybuns

Back in 2001, Emma Goss-Custard arrived in Dorset armed only with her mother's and grandmother's recipes and the goal to produce a wide range of delicious, handmade gluten-free cakes and biscuits. Fast-forward over a decade and Emma's cakes have been honoured with an array of prestigious awards, not only for their heavenly taste, but also for their careful use of natural ingredients and low environmental impact. As Honeybuns expanded, Emma decided to share her fabulous corner of south-west England with those wanting to enjoy a romantic glamping getaway. And as all good bakers do, Emma has very much risen to the occasion (sorry, couldn't resist!). Tucked away among sweeping hills is the Honeybuns vintage caravan, sleeping two adults. Don't let the term 'caravan' put you off: this is a truly unique abode as there's hardly any of these 'Arks' available for hire in England. Noah himself would be charmed by the attention to detail of this well-constructed, cosy accommodation, which comes furnished with an oversized double bed, a fully equipped kitchen area, hot water and a bathroom with free-standing loo, roll-top bath with shower, and a washbasin. Traditional campers who want to spread out beyond the caravan are also welcome to pack their canvas and pitch up close by, marvelling at the panoramic views towards the unspoiled Bulbarrow Hill.

Honeybuns, Naish Farm, Stony Lane, Holwell, Dorset DT9 5LJ 01963 23597
honeybuns.co.uk/Glamping

✿ One vintage caravan that sleeps 2 adults in an oversized double bed (contact Emma for more than 2 people). Fully equipped kitchen area, hot water, microwave, cutlery, crockery and toaster. Sole use of the bathroom with bath, shower, loo and sink. Bedding and towels provided. Guests can pitch 1 small tent near the caravan, if required. The site also has swing benches, a rose garden, open fire, chickens to feed, a resident donkey, lots of bird life, owls and bats – plus a pop-up shop.

✿ Honeybuns is only 15 miles from the historic market town of Dorchester, where you get two locations for the price of one: firstly, a genuine county town, and secondly, Thomas Hardy's fictional Casterbridge. Born just outside Dorchester, Hardy clearly used it to add credibility to his work, so much so that his literary locations can be found among the town's delightful white Georgian terraces. Dorchester is also home to some incredibly varied museums including the Dinosaur Museum (01305 269880), the Teddy Bear Museum (01305 266040) and the much acclaimed Tutankhamun Exhibition (01305 269571).

✿ There's an onsite pop-up shop open the first Saturday in the month selling Honeybuns cakes, cookies, home baking mixes, books and gifts. Honeybuns can supply local honeys, jam, chutney, cheese, breads, fruit and gluten-free items. There are several good pubs in the area, including one – The White Hart (01963 23301) – you can reach on a footpath from the site (3 miles each way across the fields. There's also the Three Elms Inn (01935 812881) and The Digby Tap (01935 813148) in Sherborne.

✿ Open April–Oct (Fri and Sat only).

✿ Price per night £100 –£135 (based on 2 adults).

glampotel

Glampotel, Rowlands Wait, Rye Hill, Bere Regis, Dorset BH20 7LP 0800 998 9129
glampotelbereregis.com

❋ Six 'canvas cottages', each with king-sized beds, luxury bedding, towels, bespoke wooden furniture and kitchen equipment, including a cool-box. There's also a lockable chest, camping lantern and candles, and a wind-up torch. The first box of wood for the stove is complimentary. There is an outside deck with gas BBQ. Cottages have their own outdoor en suite bathrooms with shower and composting toilet. Glampotel is located within a traditional touring park (Rowlands Wait), so there are facilities on site for laundry and washing-up and extra bathroom facilities.

❋ It's a short stroll into the village of Bere Regis, with 2 pubs and a quaint old church. The ruins of Corfe Castle (01929 481294) and its picture-postcard village are also nearby, and certainly worth a visit. The Purbeck Hills and Jurassic Coast offer excellent walking and cycling, with striking natural features like Durdle Door, peaceful Lulworth Cove and rugged Kimmeridge Bay (01929 481044), which is great for fossil hunting. Join sections of the South West Coast Path for the best of the beaches.
❋ Pre-order one of Glampotel's food hampers prior to arrival or walk to one of the 2 village pubs, the newly refurbished Drax Arms (01929 471386) or the Royal Oak (01929 471203), both of which serve good food.
❋ Open April–Sept.
❋ From £110 per night, minimum 2-night stay.

In a handsome thatched cottage built by his grandfather, Thomas Hardy penned some of his most famous works, peering from his windows across the delicate Dorset countryside beyond. It's not difficult to find Hardy's fictional county of Wessex in modern-day Dorset, and those who plod in the tracks of Tess of the D'Urbervilles can easily discover the beautiful rural hideaway of Kingsbere, known to us as Bere Regis. The 12th-century church and quaint rural pubs still have a storybook charm, while a wander into the ancient woodland reveals a setting unchanged since Hardy's time. The one true innovation in recent years around these parts has been the addition of one of Wessex's most high-end glampsites – Glampotel, a well-hidden group of six en suite 'canvas cottages', two located in a meadow and four in their own glade, all nestled close enough to the trees to have a magical woodland feel. The 'cottages' are similar in design to bell tents (in fact, four *are* bell tents) and are pitched on wooden platforms to provide a flat ground surface and deck outside which you can relax as you fire up the fancy gas BBQ. Step inside to find a king-sized bed in the centre of a large space with wooden cabinets to the side, topped with traditional candle lanterns. A wood-burning stove provides that extra rustic charm and an opportunity to stoke up the heat, so you can cocoon yourself in the warmth of your cosy abode. You can also stash away food in the cool-box provided, so your local Dorset cheese doesn't melt away while you read beside the fire!

Glampotel actually shares its space with Rowlands Wait Camping and Touring Park. You are welcome to use all the facilities the campsite provides, including the laundry and the small onsite shop, but can forgo the communal sanitary blocks in favour of your canvas cottage's own en suite bathroom. The en suites have hot showers and composting toilets, and each tent has a parking area next to its pitch. Indeed, having settled into Glampotel's canvas cottages, guests will find themselves very much separate from the touring park, and those hoping for that extra boutiquey feel can ask for one of the 'romance packages' with scented candles, wine, and chocolates, or order a delicious local hamper.

While the 300-acre ancient forest on the site's doorstep will absorb imaginative children, who can build dens and search for wildlife, those who hop back in the car will be rewarded with the best that Dorset has to offer. Beautiful Lulworth Cove and Durdle Door are a short drive away, as is Kimmeridge Bay – the latter perfect for fossil-hunting and rockpooling. Meanwhile, inland, historic Dorchester remains a point of pilgrimage for Thomas Hardy fans - or at least those who didn't get sidetracked looking for fictional Kingsbere.

bloomfield camping

A seven-acre site full of wild flowers and lily-lined ponds, Bloomfield Camping is the stunning result of the ongoing dedication, love and passion of its genial owners, Jon and Amanda. Hidden at the end of a single-track lane, the site is home to just four beautiful bell tents, each surrounded by young fruit trees that in season provide a bounty of fresh, dewy pears to enjoy with breakfast at your own canopy-covered picnic table – utterly idyllic. It's perhaps the sheer space that is the most striking thing about Green Tourism-endorsed Bloomfield (Gold award, since you asked). With a maximum of just four families staying at any one time, this is a completely different experience to the more high-density campsites common throughout Dorset, with a sense of quietness and calm that makes it feel like a secret haven, hidden from the rest of the world.

Pitched atop timber decking, each six-metre bell tent sleeps four, with a beautiful, king-size oak bed and two chairs that convert into single futon beds, bedside cabinets, rugs and lanterns; bunting and peacock feathers add a splash of style. These homely abodes are clearly well-loved, well-maintained, and have ample storage room in which to tuck away those wellies after a day of rambling in the fields, as you dry off beside the roaring firepit.

Each tent comes with a kitchenette equipped with everything you could possibly need, from crockery and cutlery to a gas oven and a cool-box refilled with newly chilled ice packs every day. It would be a shame for those ice packs to go to waste, so do make sure the cool-box is well stocked with plenty of local cider, perry and Dorset wine. A compost toilet is tucked away in the bushes on the far side of the site and, for those of you who simply can't be without hot showers and a hairdryer, there is also a brand new, solar-powered shower block on the other side of the field (complete with two flushing loos, washbasins and showers, and a phone and iPod charging station for each tent).

If you wander off to explore among the flowers and trees, you'll stumble upon some exciting finds. Beside the ponds, under a dense canopy of willow branches, a collection of hammocks tempt with the promise of an afternoon nap; children will no doubt be more interested in the rope swings that have been hung from the trees. Wander on a bit further and you may see Dave, the campsite's resident peacock, strutting his stuff among the long grass.

Beyond the site's gate, you will find tranquil walking paths beside which wild berries and mushrooms grow in abundance. A climb to the top of the Iron Age hill fort that sits just behind Bloomfield offers the perfect location to enjoy a forager's picnic while looking down upon this special spot.

Bloomfield Camping, Common Drove, Child Okeford, Poole, Dorset DT11 8QY 07766 292732
bloomfieldcamping.com

❋ Each pitch has its own kitchen unit, canopy with table and chairs, and a firepit with grate for campfire cooking. The kitchens are equipped with gas cooker with hob, grill and oven. All crockery, cutlery, pots, pans, washing-up equipment and tea towels are provided (as well as tea, coffee, etc). A large cool-box is provided for each kitchen and ice packs are exchanged daily. There are 2 flushing toilets, 2 showers and 2 washbasins. There is also a washing-up sink. Hairdryer and straighteners for use free of charge. There is also an additional waterless/compost toilet on site. Mobile phone/tablet charging available for each tent.

❋ With all of its planting, Bloomfield is a carbon-negative site and even offers a tree-planting scheme for campers wishing to offset their holiday travel.

❋ The Iron Age hill fort of Hambledon Hill is directly accessible from the site, while the ancient settlement of Badbury Rings is just 20 minutes away. For something a little more high octane, two of the country's best downhill bike centres, the UK Bike Park (07719 335076) and

Gorcombe Extreme Sports (01258 452219) are both just down the road near Blandford Forum. For the kids, the Coolplay Adventure Centre (01258 474666) boasts all manner of foamy amusements. Explore the area via the North Dorset Trailway (accessible just a mile from the site) or take to the skies for a bird's-eye view at Compton Abbas Airfield (01747 811767).

❁ Gold Hill Organic Farm Shop (01258 861916) sells local organic produce for you to cook in your onsite kitchen – it can even deliver to the site. The owners also run an organic café providing hearty Dorset meals and a fine selection of local brews. Child Okeford boasts 2 cracking pubs that are just a short stroll from the site – the Saxon Inn (01258 860310) and the Bakers Arms (01258 860260). A mobile fish and chip van stops in the village centre every Thursday. Orders can be phoned through in advance to avoid the queues. For those with more sophisticated palates, English Oak Vineyards (01258 858205) offers tours and tastings of their exceptional sparkling wines.

❁ Open end May–mid Sept.

❁ Low season: Fri–Mon £280, Mon–Fri £280. High season: Fri–Fri £620.

botany glamping

Botany Farm, Bradley Road , Warminster, Wiltshire BA12 7JY 07713 404233 botanycamping.com

❄ Six regular pitches and 16 glamping bell tents across 2 fields. Bell tents sleep up to 5. They include beds, stoves, utensils and everything you require for cooking, a firepit and solar-powered fairy lights, a free campfire pack (wood, firelighters, marshmallow, skewers) and cool-box with frozen cool blocks. You'll need to bring your own bedding and towels. There are composting toilets and flushing loos plus 4 family shower rooms with sinks and hot water.

❄ Less than 4 miles away, Longleat House and Safari Park (01985 844400) is the UK's premier wildlife experience.

Botany Manager Crispin can get you 30% off your ticket price. Travel 30 minutes north to the historic city of Bath, which is small but eloquent and a good day-trip from the campsite. A similar distance in the opposite direction takes you to Salisbury, with its towering cathedral (01722 555120) and narrow streets. Be sure to stop at Stonehenge en route.

❄ A small onsite shop sells essentials and sweet things for the kids. There are also several pubs and restaurants in Warminster. The Snooty Fox (01985 846505) is one of the closest and best.

❄ Open all year.

❄ Bell tent glamping from £100 per night.

The grand Elizabethan architecture of Longleat House vies for the public's attention with the exoticism and fun of the safari park behind. The first of its kind outside of Africa, the 500-species-strong park is kept slightly separate from the house, so those planning to admire the crystal-clad ballroom won't find monkeys on their bonnet, grasping at the windscreen wipers. On particularly still evenings, though, the roar of male lions can still be heard beyond the enclosure boundaries, carrying over the house to the surrounding Wiltshire countryside.

Beyond the range of the lions' roars and the chattering of howler monkeys lies a small campsite with a top location. Three miles from Longleat and ideally situated for exploring the rest of the county, Botany Camping is a charmingly simple campsite that also boasts a colourful cluster of bell tents for those looking for a more effortless stay. Choose this glamping option and you needn't bring much at all other than your duvet and a devil-may-care attitude. Guests will find futon-style beds, eco-fuel heaters, cooking facilities and all the utensils required, while campers and glampers alike still share the composting toilets and conventional flushing loos, along with four family shower rooms in a separate shelter.

Each pitch offers plenty of space and includes a firepit where campfires are not only allowed, but positively encouraged, with guests arriving to a thoughtful 'starter pack' including wood, firelighters, skewers and a hefty pack of marshmallows. The site also boasts a small shop at the entrance for buying essentials, while a supermarket in nearby Warminster is well placed for a larger shopping session.

The size of the campsite gives it a friendly, sociable atmosphere, but much of this is also down to the relaxed personality of Crispin, the ever-present yet unobtrusive, manager whose welcoming and helpful nature makes him the go-to man for queries of all kinds. It's no surprise, then, that such niceness has seen him charm his neighbours into offering 30% off Longleat tickets, which is very handy for family visitors.

Cycling, walking and fishing in the local countryside, along with Stonehenge, Bath and Salisbury (all 30 minutes away), makes Botany Camping a pleasant base for would-be explorers. And if you're there on a clear night you can even use the North Star to guide you. With a proper rural setting and no light pollution, this is the perfect place for admiring the stars of the night sky.

the farm camp

Fancy escaping the trappings of modern life? Perhaps family, friends or colleagues have been hinting at a countryside retreat for a special occasion? Well, swing on over to the secluded woodlands of The Farm Camp, where peace, tranquillity and fuss-free group camping awaits. There's something very special about arriving at Church Farm to find someone has already made camp for you. With beds made and stove at the ready, just bring your nearest and dearest, and some fresh supplies for a BBQ under the starry Wiltshire skies. The site's four, off-grid, self-catered bell tents (fondly named after West Country phrases: 'Wossnem', 'Eesorite', 'Yertis' and 'Ispecso') come furnished in a cosy, shabby-chic style, with über-comfortable mattresses, fresh linen, cooking and dining equipment and a wood-burning stove. Outside the attention to detail continues with well-cleared pathways leading to the showers, compost loos (much nicer than the name suggests) and the well-equipped, rustic camp kitchen shelter. Less than half a mile down the country lane, happy campers also have access to Church Farm's facilities, which include an indoor swimming pool, games room and laundry facility.

As for things to do nearby, the site is a brief stroll from the Limpley Stoke valley and the Kennet Avon canal area, which is walking, cycling and boating territory; plus the River Avon has a number of wild swimming spots with various pubs and cafés beside them. A visit to this corner of the world isn't complete, however, without a wander around Bath, just five miles away. With its splendid terraces, sweeping honey-stone crescents and fascinating array of historical sites, it's little wonder UNESCO named the whole city a World Heritage Site, boasting more listed buildings than almost anywhere else in the country, including one of the world's finest Roman spas and the opulent Royal Crescent. There are plenty of activities back at The Farm Camp, too, where guests can try their hand at the ancient art of sheep-herding. After learning the basic principles, try to direct those woollen workers around a simple course, against the clock. Other activities include archery, yoga and massage (by the multi-talented Angela) and keeping deathly silent while trying to spot 'The Big 5': deer graze nearby, foxes and badgers come out at night, buzzards hunt in the adjacent fields and then there's Big Steve, the resident farmer.

Church Farm, Winsley, Bradford-on-Avon, Wiltshire BA15 2JH 01225 582246 thefarmcamp.co.uk

❋ Four bell tents (sleeping from 12–16 in total) with ready-made beds, wood-burning stove, kettle, cooking and eating equipment in the camp kitchen and cool-box. Shared camp features include 2 hot showers and eco-friendly shower gel and compost loos. Drinking water, sink, refuse and recycling bins in the camp kitchen and car parking field. Please note that, although this is an 'off-grid' camp, power is available down the country lane in the laundry room.

❋ For activities you're welcome to try your hand at the ancient art of sheep-herding on the farm. Or take a tour around Quoins (07835 265082), a small, local, organic vineyard a mile away in Little Ashley. The last outpost of the Cotswolds, the unspoiled market town of Bradford-on-Avon, is also nearby. Often described as a 'mini Bath', the town has a wonderful collection of indie shops, restaurants and cafés lining the narrow streets of the centre.

❋ Run by cousin Tom, Hartley Farm Shop (01225 864948) offers a delicious range of home-grown and locally produced goods. Located less than half a mile away, it offers a 10% discount for camp guests, and a catering package is also available. The village Co-op has a large selection of food and drink items, along with an off-licence, newsagent and Post Office. It's also situated next to the closest bus stops to Bath and Bradford-on-Avon. The recently refurbished Seven Stars (01225 722204) is in the village of Winsley – and serves excellent food and a wide range of local cask ales and fine wines.

❋ Open Easter–Oct.

❋ From £109 per person for a 3-night weekend break and £89 per person for a 2-night midweek break.

mill farm glamping

When entering your canvas lodge you may well find an inquisitive duck inspecting your veranda or a cheeky chick taking a nap on the entrance rug. It's as if they're trying to remind you that they're the ones who really live here and not you. But this is precisely the charm of Mill Farm, which is much as it says on the tin – a fully operational organic farm with 100 heifers, 200 calves, wild geese and, of course, Moto the Mill Farm donkey. A family-run operation in the heart of rural Wiltshire, Mill Farm positively buzzes with life yet still boasts all the essentials for a perfect glamping holiday. Designed for guests wanting to reacquaint with nature without compromising on comfort, each canvas lodge is beautifully furnished, featuring a generous master bedroom, a secondary bedroom (with single beds) and a stove with an oven, hob, and wood-burning fire. Guests can also enjoy the convenience of a piping-hot shower and flushing toilet on the rear deck, while out front the dining area opens on to the covered veranda. All that local produce somehow tastes even better in the fresh country air.

It's the newest addition to the farm that is the biggest highlight, however. Perfect for the pages of *Guinness World Records*, the farm's specially made 'squirrel lodge' – a two storey safari tent – is the first and currently only one of its kind in the UK. The stylish design replicates the other four lodges on site, but the extra space allows for a sumptuous four-poster bed downstairs and another two bedrooms up above, partitioned by beautifully crafted wooden walls. The result is ample space for a big family getaway without having to reduce the size of the kitchen or living areas.

Outside, Mill Farm can feel like the middle of nowhere (which is one of its draws) but, in reality, civilisation is surprisingly close, with plenty of fascinating attractions to keep you busy. Avebury rivals (and some would say exceeds) Stonehenge as England's most impressive pre-historic site. Spared from its neighbour's commercialism, its visitors are able to meander freely among its mysterious stones, which date back to 3000 BC. For visitors who just can't resist that Stonehenge photo opportunity, you're in luck; the iconic and much-loved monument is only a half-hour drive away.

One of the farm's real delights has to be the surrounding wildlife. Rabbits, deer, foxes, kingfishers, and kestrels can all be spotted from the comfort of your lodge. One animal less likely to make an appearance is the badger, but Chris, Izzy and Joe have introduced their very own watching hide so guests have the rare opportunity to get up close to these night-loving creatures while the rest of Wiltshire is tucked up in bed.

**Mill Farm Glamping, Belle Vue Farm, Poulshot,
Devizes, Wiltshire SN10 1RZ 01380 828351
millfarmglamping.co.uk**

❀ The lodges have everything you need, including
showers and toilets, a kitchen, dining area,
wood-burning stove with oven and very comfy beds.

❀ Inside one of Mill Farm's old barns, an honesty
shop stocks fresh bread, butter, milk, cakes, cheeses,
quiches, and local sausages, bacon, chicken and beef
to cook on your stove. There's a clipboard for
recording purchases and you settle up at the end of
your stay. Make sure you check out the blackboard
detailing events taking place on the farm; it's
updated daily and includes info on free farm tours,
donkey rides, horseriding and other activities. There's
also a straw play arena that offers fun for the kids
whatever the weather.

❀ Bowood House Gardens (01249 812102), home
of the Marquis and Marchioness of Landsdowne,
offers a fantastic family day out and is home to a
treasure trove of fascinating items. Its grounds are a
peaceful break from the hectic adventure
playground. For real history, visit Stonehenge. It is
near Salisbury in the lovely Wiltshire countryside,
the highlight of any trip to Wiltshire.

❀ A 15-minute walk up Poulshot Road takes you to
The Raven Inn (01380 828271), a charming pub with
traditional decor and good-quality grub. If the sun's
shining, head to The Rowdey Cow Café Ice Cream
Parlour (01380 829666) for fresh ice cream made on
the farm, seating in the garden and a play area for
the kids.

❀ April –end Oct.

❀ Midweek stays from £200 (for 2 nights in low
season); weekends from £420; weekly rates
from £520.

red squirrel glamping

They've long been our political allies, but one group of Americans is less welcome in the British countryside these days: grey squirrels, which are pretty much everywhere and have famously driven out our native red species. The Isle of Wight, however, can claim itself as the last island fortress of red squirrels. Here they thrive in the untainted natural landscape, particularly on the Hamstead Heritage Coast, where nature reserves and farmland pepper a landscape perforated by river estuaries.

With wildlife thriving and farm tractors trundling down the track, the aptly named Red Squirrel Glamping makes the most of this idyllic island location. Perched in a quiet corner of Hamstead Farm, this tasteful new addition to the landscape is an enviable place to spend a night or three and, with the two safari tents of Red Squirrel Glamping already pitched, all you need do is turn up and light the BBQ. Sleeping up to seven people, these well-furnished abodes have a double room with king-sized bed, a separate room with bunk bed and trundle bed, and a foldable day bed in the living space. Despite this, there is still ample space in the rest of the tent, with a

well-kitted kitchen that has all the utensils and crockery you need, along with a comfortable family area with a toasty wood-burning stove. Throughout it all, hosts Simon and Victoria have added thoughtful touches like books, games and a welcome hamper on arrival that shows the care and attention they have put into the campsite's creation.

Out the back there's a private bathroom with a proper flushing loo and a modern shower unit. From within its wooden walls you can still just about hear the call of the cockerel as you take your morning shower. Indeed, the chickens really are your closest neighbours, with a coop from which you can collect eggs for breakfast. Cows and horses are also close at hand, and among the trees you might see a pheasant or even a red squirrel. Stroll further and you'll stumble across the farm's secluded stony beach. On a warm sunny day, it's a great place to sit while children hunt for fossils and you gaze at the sailing boats drifting across the horizon.

The rest of the Isle of Wight is probably what you're rushing to explore, but Red Squirrel Glamping will make you pause for thought. As you watch the ebb and flow of the tide from your wooden veranda, the pace of life here slows to that languid holiday rhythm we're all looking for.

Hamstead Farm, Hamstead Drive, Yarmouth, Isle of Wight PO41 0YE 07968 396765
redsquirrelglamping.co.uk

❁ Tents sleep up to 7, with bedding and towels provided. A fully equipped kitchen has a gas hob, fridge, plus all the utensils and crockery required. A lounge area has a wood-burning stove complete with an oven. An outside veranda has a BBQ and, at the back of each tent, there is a private bathroom with flushing loo and shower.

❁ The Newtown National Nature Reserve (01983 531785) is an estuary and conservation area of mudflats, salt marsh and meadows. From the visitor point opposite the Old Town Hall, a gentle mile-and-a-half walk takes you around the village and church of Newtown and out to the old quay and salt-pan feeder ponds where salt was made until the 1930s.

❁ The nearest pub is the Horse & Groom (01983 760672), 1.5 miles away – a family-friendly spot with an extensive garden and outdoor play area. The New Inn (01983 531324) is also relatively close at hand and has one of the best reputations on the island for food.

❁ Open March–Oct.

❁ From £100–£160 per night. Minimum stay 3 nights (peak) and 2 nights (off peak).

adhurst yurts

Adhurst Yurts, Adhurst Estate, Petersfield, Hampshire GU31 5AD 07789 954476 adhurst.co.uk

❀ Four yurts and 1 coppicer's cabin (with its own open-roofed shower and long-drop privy), 1 gas-heated shower deck big enough for the whole family, 3 long-drop toilets, 2 flushing toilets and an indoor wet room. Guests in Willow yurt have an en suite bath tub. There are 4 safari kitchens and a veranda kitchen with the cabin. Excellent fly-fishing on the River Roth, a rope swing on its banks, a zip wire and tennis court all provide onsite fun. Regular bushcraft courses with a qualified local team.

❀ In the heart of the South Downs National Park, there's a wealth of walking trails nearby, not least the famous South Downs Way. In the local village of Petersfield a small boating pond hires out rowing boats and canoes. The Watercress Line Steam Railway (01962 733810) offers a unique way to enjoy the Hampshire countryside, and both Gilbert White's House (01420 511275) and the fabulous National Trust-owned Woolbeding Gardens (0844 249 1895) are not far from the line.

❀ You can pre-order a 'Stew for Two' (£25), or enjoy the 'Breakfast Hamper for 2' (£25), while a visiting fishmonger provides anything from dressed crab to seafood kebabs. Within pleasant walking distance through the woods, The Queens Head (01730 265489) and the award-winning Harrow (01730 262685) are two superb traditional pubs.

❀ Open Easter–Oct, with occasional winter dates.

❀ From £220 for 2-night midweek breaks, £385 for 3-night weekends. Each yurt is priced differently.

Phrases like 'back to nature' and 'authentic outdoors experience' slip off the tongue easily when you're discussing glamping, but few places more genuinely encapsulate what's special about a night under canvas than Adhurst Yurts, where rustic charm combines with comfort and luxury on the edge of an ancient woodland. A carpet of bluebells, a weaving river and leafy canopy enclose a campsite that provides the dreamiest escape imaginable from normal life – a slice of glamping wilderness just an hour from London. Amid the greenery of the South Downs National Park, this venture started out with just one cosy abode before blossoming into the four they have today. A fifth, carefully crafted wood cabin offers the same, lavish comforts along with its own en suite gas shower and toilet. Each yurt is individually designed and finished with a stylish eye for detail, complete with wood-burning stoves and spongy double beds. They're situated 100m apart and have access to one of four outdoor kitchens, including a main safari kitchen sheltered beneath a cedar wood roof. Gas hobs provide an easy boil for the morning cuppa, and come dinnertime you can make use of the site's other cooking contraptions – a bonfire tripod with hanging pot, an iron cooking stair and a cast-iron chicken roaster that keeps meat succulent and turns the mundane task of cooking into a holiday highlight. Onsite ablutions too are given a wilderness twist, with a roofless gas hot water shower that's so deep in the woods you stand beneath nothing but leaves. And those in the Willow yurt can enjoy an en suite bath in the warm glow of solar fairy lights. There are also flushing loos and a wet room by the car park. There are plenty of attractions nearby – including 'pick-your-own' Durleighmarsh Farm a mile up the road – but you don't really need to go anywhere: the 100-acre woodland is covered with paths and provides endless amusement for kids who want to build dens, whizz along the zip wire, or rope swing across the River Rother. There is also a tennis court and regular organised bushcraft courses.

knepp safaris

It all started with a vision. The 3,500 acres of the Knepp Estate, centred around a John Nash-designed castle had, for over 220 years, been devoted to arable and dairy farming. But heavy Sussex clay is particularly hostile to intensive modern farming techniques, and the farm was making an unsustainable loss. So Charlie Burrell, Knepp's owner, took a bold step and tried something radically different: rewilding. Using a mix of grazing animals to drive a mosaic of different habitats, Knepp is now a veritable Eden of biodiversity.

Herds of Exmoor ponies, Longhorn cattle, Tamworth pigs, and red and fallow deer rove at will through water meadows, open wood pasture, dynamic scrubland and dense groves of sallow. This unique environment is a magnet for wildlife like owls, bats, snakes and lizards. Rare species have found sanctuary here, too. Incredibly, Knepp is now home to 2% of the UK's population of nightingales and is a breeding hotspot for purple emperor butterflies and endangered turtle doves. The Knepp Wildland Project's expert ecologists offer a range of guided safaris looking at all these amazing species, so if you're batty about bats, or the bees get you buzzing, you can choose the tour that suits you best. If

you'd prefer a more bespoke experience, the dedicated team here will do their best to accommodate you. What could be more awe-inspiring than experiencing the wildlife up close? Camping here, that's what!

However, while the setting feels every bit as wildly exotic as the Serengeti, camping at the Knepp Estate is far from a primitive experience. There is a dizzying array of fabulous glamping abodes available, from shepherd's huts, yurts, a tipi, and bell tents of all shapes and sizes (think of it as wild camping with a small 'w'), with funky upcycled camp kitchens and luxurious hot water showers, inside and out – plus they allow campfires! As for the key ingredients for that all-important campsite BBQ, you can't get more free-range than the very livestock roaming this unspoiled, herbaceous hideaway – beautiful organic longhorn steaks, venison burgers and Tamworth sausages – available to buy on site.

Waking up to the sounds of nature is one of the great joys of camping. But the early morning call of the resident beasts at Knepp Estate offers an added thrill, reminding you that you are camping in one of the England's great mini-wildernesses, where nature reigns more harmoniously than ever.

**Knepp Safaris, New Barn Farm, Swallows Lane, Dial Post, West Sussex RH13 8NN 01403 713230
kneppsafaris.co.uk**

❋ Three shepherd's huts, 3 spacious bell tents, a huge tipi and a yurt, plus 8 smaller unfurnished bell tents, as well as some regular tent pitches. Proper flush loos, showers, compost toilets and mobile phone/laptop charging pigeon-holes in reception. The onsite communal camp kitchen includes a gas cooker, 6-ring hob, fridge/freezer with ice packs, sinks, plates, cutlery and pots and pans all available to use. Wi-Fi is available.

❋ You might find it impossible to tear yourself away from this Edenesque hideaway. However, should you want to venture forth, you can head to the charming nearby town of Rye. The Royal Military Canal (01797 367934) is just the place for a tranquil amble, while Rye Heritage Centre (01797 226696) will fill in the blanks of your local history knowledge. If stately country piles and exquisitely landscaped gardens are your thing, the National Trust's Petworth House (01798 342207), whose grounds were landscaped by Capability Brown, and the imposing pile of Arundel Castle (01903 882173), are both also worth a visit.

❋ For food and drink, look no further than Garlic Wood Farm (07903 455367), a local organic butcher that sells the Knepp Estate's beautiful 'wild-range' longhorn beef, venison and Tamworth pork. They have an outlet on the estate itself, within walking distance at Pound Farm (01403 741616), and also a shop on the High Street in Steyning.

❋ The choice of the local boozers are The Crown Inn (01403 710902) and The Countryman Inn (01403 741383) near Shipley. Both serve a range of ales and hearty pub grub.

❋ Open Easter–end of Oct.

❋ Furnished tents and huts from £75–£135 per night. Unfurnished bell tents (maximum 2 people) £30 per night plus £15 pppn. Camp beds available at £10. Breakfast baskets, firewood and charcoal all available to order too.

wild boar wood

(eco camp uk)

The team behind Eco Camp UK at Wild Boar Wood take secrecy seriously. So seriously, in fact, that the exact location of this semi-luxury campsite is only revealed upon booking. And who could blame them for wanting to keep the whereabouts of this magnificent bell tent site under wraps? For after you carefully make your way through the meandering country lanes of this particularly lovely corner of West Sussex, Eco Camp's instructions lead you to a five-acre bluebell wood that you can not only call home for the weekend, but which you quite possibly might never want to leave.

Wild Boar Wood is located right on the High Weald – a captivating Area of Outstanding Natural Beauty that spreads across a vast stretch of Kent and Sussex. The immediately surrounding 40 acres are abuzz with a rich array of woodland wildlife, from woodpeckers and butterflies to roe deer, foxes and hedgehogs. The nine bell tents that adorn the shimmering purple forest floor make for a cosy, hassle-free stay. Moreover, every aspect of your holiday has been considered with sustainability in mind, from the wood-fired showers and eco-friendly shampoos to special eco-loos that accompany more ordinary flushing toilets. It all gives the place a green edge that suits the type of 'wild glamping' it provides. But don't take our word for it; get the secret password to find out for yourself…

Eco Camp UK, Wild Boar Wood, Horsted Keynes, West Sussex RH17 7EA 0800 612 7390 ecocampuk.co.uk

✿ Nine pre-erected 'wild glamping' bell tents raised on removable decking that sleep 2–4 adults or 2 adults and 2–3 kids. They include beds, carpet, coffee table and lantern and each tent comes with its own cooking implements, cool-box, BBQ tools, chairs, table and tableware. Outside the tents you'll find a picnic table, firepit and grill for cooking with an allocation of fire wood. There are also gas-fired showers and unique hot-water bucket-showers, plus regular flushing toilets.

✿ Wild Boar Wood is located right on the High Weald – a designated AONB. Ashdown Forest is nearby, famously known as the home of Winnie the Pooh, and the area has an enviable array of walks and cycle routes. Should you wish to explore in a more laid-back way, the Bluebell Railway (01825 720800) is a charming steam locomotive that travels to East Grinstead from the National Trust property of Sheffield Park & Garden (01825 790231) – designed by Capability Brown and well worth a visit in its own right. Borde Hill (01444 450326), another magnificent set of gardens, is also close by and also worth a look – it's around a 5-minute drive from the site.

✿ There are two great pubs within a mile and a half of Wild Boar Wood. The Sloop Inn, Scaynes Hill (01444 831219) is a classic country pub serving good pub food using locally sourced produce, as is the Green Man in Horsted Keynes (01825 790656) – a quintessentially English hostelry right on the village green, which also does decent food. Foodies could also visit the award-winning High Weald Dairy (01825 791636), where they run excellent cheese-making courses.

✿ Open late April–Oct.

✿ Bell tent rates (for 2 people) £90 per night at weekends (2 night minimum); midweek nights £65. You pay more for extra children and adults.

beech estate woodland

(eco camp uk)

Eco Camp UK, Beech Estate Woodland Campsite, Beech Estate, Netherfield Hill, Battle, East Sussex TN33 0LL 0800 612 7390 ecocampuk.co.uk

❋ Eight bell tents each comfortably sleeping 2–4 adults. Inside, you'll find beds, a carpet, coffee table and lanterns. Each tent is located in its own woodland glade and comes complete with cooking implements, cool-box, BBQ tools, chairs, table and tableware. Outside the tents you'll find a wooden picnic table, firepit and grill for cooking. The site also has gas-fired showers and their unique hot water bucket showers beneath the trees, plus eco-loos and flushing toilets.

❋ Beech Estate lies right in the heart of East Sussex, a short drive from the historic town of Battle (1066, and all that) and just 3 miles away from boho Hastings. A few miles down the A271 you'll find the historic village of Herstmonceux, where there is plenty to see. Besides its historic windmill (01323 833311) it boasts the Observatory Science Centre (01323 832731) and the Tudor opulence of Hertmonceux Castle (01323 833816).

❋ The White Hart Inn in Netherfield (01424 838382) serves up classy pub grub in a truly beautiful location. Visitors can also expect a friendly welcome and great fresh seafood at the nearby Netherfield Arms (01424 838282). The Squirrel Inn in Battle (01424 772717) serves good food and a good selection of ales (including local tipple Harvey's) and hosts live music every month.

❋ Open April–Oct.

❋ Bell tent prices for 2 people: £90 per weekend night with a 2 night minimum stay; £75 for 2 people per midweek night. You pay more for extra children and adults.

There's camping, and then there's off-grid camping. Eco Camp UK's Beech Estate is most definitely the latter – no electricity, no mobile phone signal and a wheelbarrow for transporting your gear through the trees to your tent. If that all sounds like too much to cope with, then you may just want to turn the page in search of something more suitable. If it sounds like the perfect escape, you're in for a real treat. Beech Estate is the second campsite from off-grid specialists Eco Camp UK (the other is a bell-tent-only affair at Wild Boar Wood in West Sussex, see p.74), a beautiful site whose 600 acres of woodland are designated for the exclusive use of Beech Estate guests to walk, mountain bike and generally run wild. You can bring your own tent if you want to but the main event is the 'wild-glamping' bell tents they have permanently located here – each of which is sited in its own enchanting glade and comes complete with beds, chairs, a picnic table, cookware, a firepit (plus firewood) and an eco-cooking stove. It's fair to say these are functional rather than luxuriously appointed, but that's just what you'd expect in this off-grid, back-to-basics paradise and once you're here you really wouldn't want it any other way.

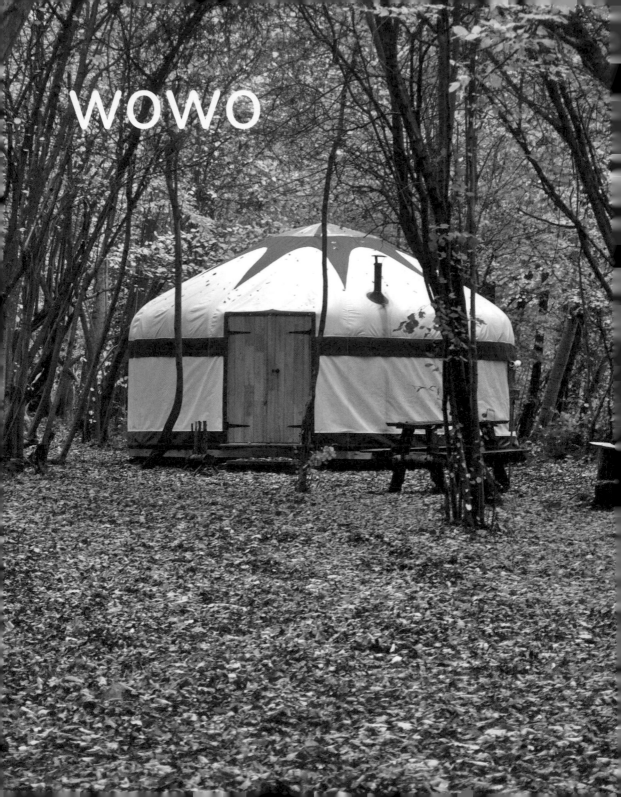
WOWO

Wapsbourne Manor Farm, or 'Wowo', as it's affectionately known by a growing band of regulars, is a rare and beautiful thing – a great campsite within two hours' drive of London. It's light on unnecessary rules and regulations, and big on fun and freedom. With smoky campfires (facilitated by a firewood delivery-man who appears at dusk on his little tractor), old rope swings and free camping for performing musicians, this is not a site for the Nanny-State-obsessed. But go with the flow and this rural wonderland is the perfect outdoor adventure playground.

This magical spot always seems to have something new to reveal: another field hidden behind the thicket, a secret pathway, a yurt nestled among the trees...There are three main areas with regular camping pitches along with a premium woodland camping area, the 'Tipi Trail', where there are more secluded places to pitch, as well as with three of the site's four yurts and two of its three shepherd's huts. The site also has a couple of gypsy caravans and two roomy lotus bell tents, plus a separate covered cooking area.

There's always something fun going on at Wowo during summer weekend evenings: soup suppers, pizza-making and plenty of mingling. Children's entertainment is strictly of the old-school variety – climbing trees, swinging on tyres, rolling around in ditches, making camps in the undergrowth. In fact, the entire 150-acre site is a huge, natural adventure playground that extends well beyond the four main camping areas. Saturday night is music night, when all-comers can join in a sing-song around the fire. Nearby, the Bluebell Railway steam train is a big draw, as is Sheffield Park, arguably one of the country's finest gardens. With four lakes forming its centrepiece, the park exudes vibrant explosions of colour at any time of the year. In autumn, black tupelos blend with the rusty reds of the maple and scarlet oak leaves; spring brings a riot of daffodils and iconic Sussex bluebells, while in summer there are flashy splodges of pink rhododendrons and the soft magenta of azaleas. Cricket fans might also care to know that the park's pitch was the venue for the first ever home tie between England and Australia in 1884.

But then, many weekend visitors don't get that far, happy to settle for the pleasures of exploring Wowo's grounds for a few days. With the evening air scented with campfire smoke, the soft murmur of sociability and perhaps a musical soundtrack, this wonderful woodland hideaway just oozes low-fi style. Leave the rules at home. Let the kids roam free.

Wowo (Wapsbourne Manor Farm), Sheffield Park, East Sussex TN22 3QT 01825 723414 wowo.co.uk

✿ Four yurts, 2 shepherd's huts and 2 lotus bell tents with a covered cooking area. 4 flushing compost toilets and 2 showers plus pot-washing in the Tipi Trail area; 4 flushing compost toilets (1 accessible) plus pot-washing in Lower Moat; 2 shower blocks with family wet rooms plus pot-washing near Lower and Middle Brook. A communal barn has ping-pong, a piano, communal fridges and freezers, Wi-Fi, an honesty bookshelf and coin-operated laundry.

✿ There are lots of activities on offer – visit Wowo's website for bushcraft, wild pottery, astronomy, ukulele, circus skills... there's even a Fairy Preservation Society! Bear in mind that this is a busy site in summer so it won't suit everybody, but for a fun, buzzy campsite where it's easy to meet fellow campers, it's hard to beat.

✿ Go for a wander around the beautiful National Trust landscaped gardens at Sheffield Park (01825 790231), just up the road. Kids can run about, feed the swans and ducks by the lake and enjoy the children's trail.

✿ Wowo's shop sells organic eggs, veg, herbs, local milk and meats plus fresh sourdough bread and loads of locally sourced goodies, including craft ales and cider. There are 2 excellent pubs neaby: the Michelin-rated Coach & Horses in Danehill (01825 740369) and the Griffin Inn in Fletching (01825 722890).

✿ Glamping open all year.

✿ Two-night stays: yurts £112–£250, shepherd's huts £124–£160, bells £156–£200, gypsy wagons £124–£160.

glottenham

There's glamping, and then there's Glottenham. Sat atop a hill overlooking the High Weald Area of Outstanding Natural Beauty, this ancient 160-acre family-run farm was once a seat of English nobility. The original Glottenham Castle was built in the 13th century as the fortified manor house of one Robert de Etchingham. The castle disappeared over time but the site went on to attract writers, artists and various dreamers to what is a magical spot, including the pre-Raphaelite poet Christina Rossetti who rhapsodised its "greenness and flowers to refresh our London eyes". The aristocrats and artists may have long since gone, but the elegantly wild beauty of Glottenham remains and is more accessible then ever because, nestled within 20 acres of ancient hornbeam woodland, Glottenham's enterprising owners Emma and Rob have created four luxurious lodgings of staggering loveliness and ingenuity. In homage to its namesake, the secluded Rossetti yurt is pure Victorian eccentricity bedecked with sunflowers, embroidered quilts and oriental rugs, and housing a gorgeous double antique bed.

The de Glottyngham geodesic dome is a cosy cocoon of shabby chic, with merino-wool bedclothes and quirky scatter cushions. On a lush verdant hillside just outside the forest, the new Bodichon yurt is decked out with vintage French linen and other cutesy features, in pure vintage style. The views over the wildflower meadow and the farm below are picture-postcard perfect. The lord of the manor here, though, is De Etchyngham. Occupying the woodland's most enviously secluded spot, this hi-spec, über-luxurious dome boasts expansive views from the decking over 20 acres of barley and wildflowers – the perfect romantic retreat.

The setting is simply breathtaking, but there's also real substance to what Emma and Rob are doing at Glottenham. Woodland and conservation courses are taught at their Forest School; all firewood and charcoal is home-produced and sustainable; and they're in the process of creating a wetland area to revive the farm's medieval fishing lakes, which also serves as the perfect view for their summer-only 'Family Fields' yurts and wild glamping site – another feather in the Glottenham cap. With big plans afoot and weekends booked up well in advance, if you haven't already booked your stay at Glottenham, you'd best get your skates on.

Glottenham, Bishops Lane, Robertsbridge, East Sussex TN32 5EB 07865 078477 glottenham.co.uk

❁ Two yurts and 2 geo-domes. Other furnished and semi-furnished units available in their 'Family Fields' during August. Composting toilets and large outdoor showers, with wash stands, plus a separate washing area for the De Etchyngham dome. No electric hook-up, but you can hire a Bio-lite Stove that converts heat into electricity for USB devices. All bedding/towels supplied. Each unit has gas cookers and firepits for campfire/BBQ. Wood-fired clay ovens for use, and the yurts and domes have wood-burning stoves. Forest School teaches foraging, herbal medicine, bushcraft skills and more. Spa treatments can be arranged. Extra 'hangout' 24ft yurt with sofas, beanbags, games and books. Firewood, charcoal and local produce hampers available.

❁ The historic town of Battle is just down the road, where you can visit the famous abbey and battlefield (01424 775705). Nearby Hastings Old Town is a charming, artsy community – and home to the largest beach-launched fishing fleet in Europe. The black, angular lines of the adjacent Jerwood Gallery (01424 728377) of modern art provides a pleasing contrast.

❁ There is a wealth of artisan farm shops nearby – Poppinghole Farm (01580 880503), Buster's (01580 882020) – with its own butchery – and a little further afield Catsfield's Great Park Farm (01424 772531) are among the best. Robertsbridge is similarly sorted for fabulous pubs. The George Inn (01580 880315) is a welcoming, family-friendly inn with an inventive menu of pub grub favourites, while The Ostrich (01580 881737), with its quirky tropical garden and the Salehurst Halt (01580 880620), are also decent shouts.

❁ Open Easter–Oct.

❁ Three-night weekend/4-night midweek breaks from £325 (yurts) or £375 (geodesic domes). 'Family Field' yurts from £400 and wild glamping from £275.

the original hut
company

Just over an hour's drive or train journey
from London, in the East Sussex village of
Bodiam, The Original Hut Company
provides the perfect romantic retreat from
the hustle and bustle of city life. Tucked away
beside a sprawling apple orchard, amid an
enchanting woodland that bursts with
bluebells in spring, are four glamp-tastic
shepherd's huts. Built from recycled and
reclaimed materials (an old caravan chassis
and local wood, to be precise), these cute
glamping abodes are designed to be
sustainable and of minimal environmental
impact. However, despite their eco-
credentials, the Original Hut Company
doesn't compromise on comfort (this is
luxury camping after all). The lovingly
decorated huts (think 'shabby-chic') are a
comforting cocoon of cosiness thanks to
their wood-burning stoves, while solar
energy provides the lighting for camping
couples. There are even gas hobs and separate
huts with pristine showers and eco loos. Fires
(in the designated firepits) are positively
encouraged here. In the autumn, there's no
sweeter aroma than the smell of windfallen
chestnuts roasting on the many campfires
which fills the soothing country air.

As befitting its green philosophy, the 200-
acre Quarry Farm site is bursting with wildlife.

Nestled lovingly within an ancient coppice clearing, the site is teeming with an array of woodland creatures, including squirrels, pheasants, woodpeckers, badgers and fallow deer. Keep your eyes peeled for buzzards, too, hovering on warm thermals of air overhead. The River Rother, which meanders through the farm, attracts egrets, herons and kingfishers. Guests are welcome to fish and splash about. Barn owls use the bottom of the farm as a hunting ground and there are beehives in the orchards. There's even a summer forest school for the your little pioneers, so they can venture out at twilight looking for the various animals.

Friendly owners, Nick and Anna Eastwood are the very personification of hospitality and are eager to make your stay as hassle-free as possible, and so food hampers and catered meals can be delivered to the site by arrangement. Or, if you're looking for a true 'back-to-nature' experience, they occasionally run foraging courses during autumn in conjunction with the nearby Michelin-starred Curlew restaurant (one of several courses offered on site). All this, plus fairytale Bodiam Castle just a short stroll away. What more could you ask for?

The Original Hut Company, Quarry Farm, Bodiam, East Sussex TN32 5RA 01580 831 845 original-huts.co.uk

---

❀ Eight shepherd's huts plus woodland camping at sister site Hop Pickers Wood. There is a wash hut with 2 loos and 2 showers. Off-grid, but lighting is provided by solar power and heating by wood-burning stoves. Each hut is kitted with a fully equipped kitchen area including gas hob, sink and cool-boxes. There's a dining area which folds out to form a double bed, plus a sofa/kid's bed and fold-out bunk sleeping 2. A communal covered cook house is also provided. Campfires are permitted in the firepits. Ask Anna about the onsite spa for manicures, facials and other treatments; various other activities on offer include kayaking, paddleboarding, archery and wild swimming, all located within the site grounds.

❀ National Trust-run Bodiam Castle (01580 830196) is a 15-minute stroll across the fields, and is worth visiting for the views from its towers alone. Boat trips (01797 253838) run from the castle down the river to a nearby pub, The White Hart (01797 252166) in Newenden. Kids will love the Kent & East Sussex Railway (01580 765155), a steam train that runs from the farm and through the Rother Valley to Tenterden in Kent.

❀ Catered meals can be prearranged and there is a small shop on site. The area is a real foodie hub, with several decent country pubs in the vicinity plus countless food festivals including nearby Rye's famous Wild Boar Week and Rye Bay Scallop Week every Easter. Pub-wise, the Castle Inn (01580 830330) is just the other side of the river and serves good food. Or try the Curlew restaurant (01580 861394), a 2-mile walk away, which is amazingly affordable for a Michelin-starred restaurant.

❀ Open all year except Jan and Feb.

❀ Huts from £82 per hut per night; £325 for a peak-season break. A surcharge of £7pp applies to all stays, to cover bed linen and firewood.

gooseberry
field campsite

**Gooseberry Field Campsite, Thorne House, Smarden Road, Pluckley, Kent TN27 0RE 07788 237588
gooseberryfieldcampsite.com**

☀ Five luxury bell tents, each furnished with a double futon bed and 2 single futons with bedding and each with their own theme; also 3 'Just a Tent' bell tents; a retro 1970s caravan; and a luxury tipi that is used as a communal space. All of the glamping pitches feature deck chairs, a picnic table, a firepit with a BBQ cooking plate and a Dutch oven. Gas camping cookers are available on request. All cooking utensils are provided (cutlery, crockery, etc) and each pitch has a cool-box. Tents are dressed with tea light chandeliers or fairy lights, lanterns, cushions, throws and blankets, board games and 2 bedside tables. The 'Just a Tent' pitches come with a firepit and a couple of lanterns. There are no electrical hook-ups but on the terrace there's a waterproof area with outdoor sockets to charge iPads, phones and so on. The terrace is also home to a wood-fired brick oven, a smoker and a charcoal fired BBQ, and there's a freezer in the workshop. There is also a lovely wood-fired hot tub plus 2 showers, 1 flushing toilet and 1 eco toilet.

✿ The village of Pluckley, 15 minutes' walk away, is a small, traditional spot with a Post Office and grocery store, a butcher, a church and a decent pub – the Black Horse (01233 841948), which serves good food. It's known also for its typical round-arched Pluckley windows, which are supposed to bring good luck – though oddly it's also known as 'the most haunted village in England'!

✿ A breakfast hamper with locally produced products can be requested on booking. The campsite also has a great farm shop a couple of minutes' walk away – Pluckley Farm Shop (01233 840400) – which sells a wide range of excellent locally sourced food. Pub-wise, the Rose & Crown (01233 840048) is a couple of minutes' drive or a 25-minute walk away and serves excellent food, while the Dering Arms (01233 840371) is a lovely gastropub, with food that's a cut above the norm.

✿ Open early May–mid Sept.

✿ Luxury bell tents for the weekend: 2 people £225; 3 people £235; 4 people £245; 5 people £255. 'Just a Bell' for the weekend is £75, maximum 4 people.

Having left Shoreditch and their city jobs three years ago, John and Kerstin describe themselves as, 'aging post-punk hippies' but, while Gooseberry Field may be so laid-back it's almost horizontal, you don't have to be a seasoned Glastonbury-goer to appreciate what the couple offer here. Set in the grassy meadow remains of what was once an ancient apple orchard, Gooseberry Field Camping is the realisation of their long-term dream to head out into the countryside, enjoy the most local of local produce and chill out beneath the stars beside a roaring campfire. A convenient 15-minute drive or taxi journey from Ashford International Station (or 1 hour and 20 minutes from London); this is a campsite in the heart of Kent that still boasts easy connections to highfalutin life in central London.

No matter where you're coming from, though, Gooseberry Field offers a true escape into rural seclusion. Comprising five lovingly furnished bell tents, a tipi and a vintage 1970s caravan, it's a place that very much appeals to all tastes and budgets. Those with their own bells are also welcome and, if you fancy the glamping style but don't want every trimming, you can even rent a tent without the interior furnishings.

Whatever you choose, the comforts at Gooseberry Field extend far beyond a well-made bed. Spread around a five-acre field, the campsite drops down a grassy tier to where a raised, south-facing terrace provides space to kick back in the sun or enjoy the sparkly night sky. Most dawdling at this spot is done while someone stokes the

wood-fired hot tub a short walk away. There's no denying it's one of the site's quirky treasures, a real luxury for any camping holiday.

In keeping with the *Good Life* aspirations of anyone moving out of London, there's an element of agricultural activity here. Pigs provide sausages and bacon for breakfasts, chickens provide eggs, a small veg patch bursts with seasonal produce and, beside the terrace, a herb garden means you can garnish your barbecued goodies with freshly picked rosemary. The ancient orchard is also being restored. Though almost all of the original apple trees are gone, the few remaining provide ample produce for homemade cider each autumn, and John and Kerstin have now planted a further 150 trees along with

the cluster of gooseberry bushes that gives the site its name.

It's no surprise, then, that cooking is a fairly central part of life here and not the usual hindrance to a rural camping trip. Nice touches like cool-boxes and Dutch ovens at every pitch mean you're well set up to tackle proper campfire recipes, while on the terrace a large wood-fired oven is perfect for cooking pizzas or slow-roasting dishes overnight. There's also a charcoal BBQ and a superb hot smoker, available for all to use.

Beyond the campsite the quaint village of Pluckley has a tiny grocery store and a proper butchers, plus there's a handy farm shop. With all that on the doorstep you could easily stay the weekend and never need the car!

elmley nature reserve

Kingshill Farm, Sheerness, Kent ME12 3RW 07786 333331 elmleynaturereserve.co.uk

❀ Three shepherd's huts (each sleeping 2). Children can be accommodated in bell tents with blow-up mattresses next to the parents' hut. Each hut has an en suite with gas-heated shower, basin and loo. One hut (Vanellus) has an oil radiator, while the others feature wood-burning stoves with a hot plate top. There's a communal gas BBQ in the farmhouse garden and a kitchen complete with butler sink, gas hobs, fridge, cutlery and utensils. Inside each hut there are board games, cards and books, plus a set of binoculars. Tea, coffee and fresh milk are also provided in each hut. The campsite can either supply a breakfast in bed (£15 for 2) or deliver a 2-course supper to your hut (£18 per person).

❀ The Nature Reserve has 11 miles of trails and is a protected area, so guests are not permitted to roam freely across the marsh (maps provided). There is plenty to keep you busy on the Nature Reserve, as well as helping out on the working farm. Wildlife trails lead to 4 different bird-watching hides and a collection of other footpaths lead you to the old Victorian ruins of a former village. There are also arranged tours, walks and wildlife photography on offer if you want something a little more organised.

❀ Off the Reserve, sailing and watersports are available at nearby Barton's Point Coastal Park (07909 994196). It's a 25-minute drive to the historic town of Faversham and about the same time to wonderfully well-preserved Leeds Castle (01622 765400).

❀ Brambledown Farmshop (01795 877977) is a 10-minute drive away. It's a proper rural farm shop with great fruit, vegetables and meat. For fresh fish, visit Queenborough Harbour in the early morning to get the catch of the day. Pub-wise, the 2-mile entry road means everywhere is at least 10 minutes in the car: the Ship (01795 520881) in Conyer or the Ferry House Inn (01795 510214) are the closest places to eat and drink; both are around a 20-minute drive.

❀ Open all year.

❀ Shepherd's huts £90–£120 per night. £65 for the extra bell tent.

Elmley Nature Reserve is a painter's paradise. From your perch on a bank of raised ground in the middle of the marshland, your eyes wander across swathes of meadow grasses, catching every colour of the morning sun. In the distance, yachts glide slowly up the Swale, their movement silent and serene, while in the foreground is a peppering of geese and wildfowl, who frolic in the reed beds that front a mass of tidal streams and marshland. For the more amateur hand it's little short of a nightmare... to capture it seems simply impossible. Thankfully, from inside one of the reserve's three handcrafted shepherd's huts, the windows do the work for you – framing the outside world like a moving picture from

Harry Potter. They let the outside in, achieving a sense of true abandonment in the middle of the wetland landscape, while a lovingly decorated interior and comfy beds ensure real warmth and that cosy, hideaway feel. Be you painter, shepherd or just London-escapee, you'll feel at home here.

Nestled on the edge of a quaint farm, Elmley's secluded glamping site is a rare and wonderful thing. Despite being a National Nature Reserve, an SSSI, a Special Protected Area for birds and a 'Ramsar' site (wetlands of world importance), it's all still owned and run by the central family farm under the current tenure of Georgina and Gareth Fulton. The result is not only a reserve with boardwalks, bird-hides and informative visitor signage, but also a strikingly diverse business, from the continued importance of farming (expect to slalom through cows as you follow the two-mile drive from the entrance) to the glamping accommodation itself, an unusual privilege in such an important protected landscape. There are a small number of rules as a result – you can't go right down to the water's edge, you must stick to the marked footpaths, and public visitors are also welcome on the reserve by day – but it's rules such as these that make the place special. To stay here is to fully immerse yourself in the natural environment.

The accommodation is far from an afterthought. Located loosely around the central farm buildings, the three shepherd's huts have their own private patches and contain all you need inside to feel wonderfully self-sufficient. Each also has its own piping-hot gas-powered shower and loo. Within easy walking distance, a tall Victorian pitch-pine barn houses a communal space, with a dining table and honesty bar, books and board games, while between the huts you'll find a communal kitchen and BBQ with stunning views. It's a thoroughly welcome touch, which adds a somewhat safari feel to the experience – aided by the fact that Gareth does actually give tours of the reserve in his 4x4 if you enquire!

In the end, though, it's up to you to decide what sort of holiday you are after. You can help collect eggs from the farm chickens, watch for wading birds in one of the hides, cycle through nearby historic villages, or simply hide yourself away in the romantic setting of your hut as you watch the sun rise through the dawn mist or drift off to sleep to the sound of barn owls hooting softly across the marshes.

west stow pods

Ever fancied a glamping break in Suffolk? Well picture this – a lush, magical woodland of olive-green teeming with fabulous walks and cycling paths; a rural English landscape of gentle hills, lush valleys and delightful villages; and, finally, one of the UK's most significant archaeological sites just down a country lane. Do locations get much better? Positioned deep in the heart of Suffolk, West Stow Pods is a welcoming, well-run operation that offers hassle-free camping in the most serene of surroundings.

West Stow's skilfully constructed pods are surprisingly roomy, sleeping a family of four comfortably (a couple on the double bed and two on a fold-out sofa). The immaculately maintained wet room gets top marks for design and comes kitted out with a private shower and WC – perfect for those not fancying the morning trudge to the shower block. You'll also find a well-stocked kitchenette complete with fridge, oven, microwave, tea-making facilities and toaster.

With heating, lighting and electrical points all present and correct at West Stow, these snug shelters keep nice and toasty on a chilly winter's evening. But when the weather's playing ball, guests have the luxury of their own outdoor deck complete with table, chairs and a BBQ – ideal for a spot of al fresco

West Stow Pods, Ingham Road, West Stow, Suffolk IP28 6EX 01284 728136 weststowpods.co.uk

❀ Four camping pods each with double bed, sofa bed, wet room (complete with shower and WC), kitchenette with fridge, microwave/oven, tea-making facilities and toaster, flat-screen TV (with DVD player). Heating, lighting and electrical points, dining table, chairs, outdoor decking and BBQ area. Don't forget to bring your camping gear (bedding, cooking equipment, etc).

❀ West Stow Anglo-Saxon Village and Moyse's Hall Museum (01284 758000) are less than 2 miles from West Stow. Featuring living history and event days, workshops, walks and talks, these sites and their events bring history to life. Bury St Edmunds was once home to one of medieval Europe's mightiest monasteries and has long drawn tourists for its historic ruins, shops and well-preserved and elegant old centre. markets. You can also visit one of East Anglia's largest brewers, Greene King (01284 714297), which is based here and runs regular tours of its town centre premises. and museum.

❀ There are plenty of great places to eat and drink in Bury St Edmunds, including the Bay Tree Cafe Bistro (01223 700607), where friendly, courteous staff serve good coffee and mouth-watering cakes. On the edge of the town centre, the Bury Beer House (01284 766415) has 8 pumps dedicated to cask ale and an ever-changing range of beers from local and national brewers. They also offer a selection of simple but tasty bar snacks. Closer to the site, the Organic Shop, Cafe & Bistro Shop (01284 717175) in Fornham All Saints has a blackboard menu brimming with tasty suggestions.

❀ Open all year.

❀ Pods cost £65 per night for 2 adults and first child under 3. Subsequent children £10 per night (up to the age of 15). Extra adults £20 per night (maximum of 4 adults).

dining. But no matter how ingeniously designed, well-furnished or comfortable these pods may be, they could never compare to its untouched, woodland surroundings, which are heavenly, and reason enough to come here – not to mention the deeper forest and well-marked footpaths and bridleways of Thetford Forest a little way to the north, which could keep you occupied for days. On the edge of the forest, West Stow is a quaint village well-known for its recreated Anglo-Saxon village and the Country Park that surrounds it. To the south of the site, Bury St Edmunds is just 6 miles away and well worth a visit not only for its abbey ruins, church and handsome old centre but also as a place to shop, eat and drink and stock up on supplies.

secret meadows

Suffolk is fast becoming the UK's glamping capital. The cluster of luxury glampsites scattered around England's eastern rump leave urban exiles spoiled for choice. And it isn't hard to see why. It's a rural, relatively unspoiled county, and very handy for the capital. But with such a wealth of posh pitches to choose from, it takes something pretty special to turn the head of blasé Londoners – in fact, something exactly like Secret Meadows.

Sadly 'secret' in name only now, Secret Meadows comprises six über-luxurious lodge-style tents spread across the idyllic 115-acre White House Farm. Each has a double bed and two singles, a fully equipped kitchen area with fridge and BBQ, plus loo and shower. The Gypsy's Rest caravan and a Middle-Earth themed 'Hobbit Box' are further options, tucked against brambly hedges and trees in the most secluded areas of the site. The former has been lovingly furnished in vintage style, adorned with cute little windows, a stable door, fitted cupboards and double bed (all hand-crafted). A neighbouring shepherd's hut provides extra living space, with a fully equipped traditional kitchen, gas-powered refrigerator, wood-burning range cooker/stove, private loo and shower, hot running water throughout, and a quirky built-in double cupboard bed. The 'Hobbit Box', meanwhile, is precisely what it says on the tin – an old wooden horsebox with a large wooden veranda fashioned on to the back where a horse ramp used to be, while inside, quirky oval windows and sumptuous furnishings give a modern edge to what still feels very much like fairy-tale-style accommodation. You don't have to be a Tolkien fan to appreciate its splendour.

We could, of course, go on – to tell you all about their Gold Green Tourism award, or the bespoke glamping packages on offer (bushcraft courses ranging from whittling your own knife to full-blown survival skills). There's no doubting Secret Meadows is an extremely slick operation, but that doesn't really capture the spirit of the place. No soulless set-up this; Secret Meadows oozes effortless rustic charm. The site is also positively abuzz with wildlife, with everything from dragonflies to barn owls drawn to the vibrant wildflower meadows. It comes as no surprise that you're actually staying within the designated County Wildlife Site. With the Suffolk coast just waiting to be explored, Secret Meadows' location is hard to beat. This is one secret that's well and truly out.

Secret Meadows, White House Farm Wildlife Site, Hasketon, Nr. Woodbridge, Suffolk IP13 6JP
01394 382992 secretmeadows.co.uk

❋ Six luxury lodge tents, plus Gypsy's Rest and accompanying hut (sleeps 4) and the Hobbit Box (sleeps 4). Each tent sleeps up to 6 people with a king-sized 4-poster bed, special double enclosed wooden cabin bed and 2 singles (all bedding, linen and towels provided). All accommodation features a fully equipped kitchen area with Belfast sink, slate worktop and a traditional kitchen dresser. There's a gas-powered refrigerator, BBQ, dining area with candle chandelier and a comfy sofa. Each unit has its own private loo and shower. Electric sockets are in a building onsite for guests to charge a mobile phone or use a hairdryer.

❋ The Suffolk coast is a short drive away, where the village of Orford and cosmopolitan Aldeburgh are both well worth a visit. Woodbridge too is an attractive place, with an appealing small-town vibe. Just outside Woodbridge, the important Anglo-Saxon burial mounds of Sutton Hoo, run by the National Trust, are essential visiting for budding Tony Robinsons.

❋ There's an onsite farm shop stocking a wide range of locally sourced delectables. You can also choose from a selection of food packages including a 'Breakfast Hamper', 'Slow Food Package' and a 'BBQ Box'. Of course, you can always cook your own in the traditional wood-burning range or BBQ on the Kadai. There's a wealth of great pubs and restaurants in the area. The Galley (01394 380055) in Woodbridge offers a refined menu; the excellent Anchor pub (01394 382649), close to the Woodbridge waterfront, not only does great pub meals but is a proper, cosy pub. Or try the restaurant of the Crown Hotel (01394 384242), which serves really excellent, locally sourced food from an imaginative menu.

❋ Open March–Nov.

❋ Luxury Lodge Tents from £545 for a 3-night weekend stay; from £369 for a 4-night midweek stay; from £981 for a week's stay. Gypsy's Rest and the Hobbit Box from £445 for a 3-night weekend stay; from £357 for a 4-night midweek stay; and from £779 for a week's stay.

alde garden

If there were an annual award for 'English campsite with the greatest diversity of accommodation', the owners of Alde Garden would be permanently practising their acceptance speeches and making mental notes not to blub. Guests to this peaceful campsite, situated in the garden of the excellent White Horse Inn on the edge of the tiny Suffolk village of Sweffling, can choose between a stay in a bell tent, a yurt, a gypsy caravan or a 'wooden tent on stilts' (inspired by a trip to New Zealand). Alternatively, they can simply bring along their own tent and camp in the time-honoured fashion.

Indeed, owners Marie and Mark encourage non-campers who have booked into the more glampy accommodation to bring along a tent and give traditional camping a try. Battle-hardened tentophiles, conversely, can spend their final night in the yurt or gypsy caravan as a naughty treat (there's even a cute self-catering cottage for really unenthusiastic campers). Oh, and the pub – East Anglia pub of the year in 2015, no less – is an absolute gem, with real ale, fabulous bar snacks and regular live music, plus a handy off-licence service for the campers.

Whatever accommodation you opt for, the vibe remains the same: a garden kept deliberately wild (and with its own friendly hedgehog), combined with facilities artfully constructed from reclaimed and recycled materials, engendering an appealing laid-back atmosphere.

Take the brilliant jungle shower, for example – made from wood Mark and Marie have picked up. Showerers can hitch up one of the site's bags of solar-heated water to enjoy an outdoor shower, with the added bonus of a view of next door's free-range pigs. There are also two spotless conventional showers for those to whom cleanliness is next to indoorsiness.

The pathways around the 0.89-acre site (they've measured it) weave a web of discovery, with different glamping structures and homemade wares at every corner. There's a communal kitchen area in a wooden barn, complete with straw bale seats – a particular hit with kids – plus a well-stocked bookcase in the yurt. A friend of the couple created the wood-burning stoves from discarded gas bottles. And if you're more into cycling than recycling, you can borrow one of a cluster of bikes, including a tandem, kept on site, and strike into the deepest rural Suffolk countryside beyond.

Alde Garden, The White Horse Inn, Low Road, Sweffling, Suffolk IP17 2BB 01728 664178 aldegarden.co.uk

✤ Two yurts, 1 gypsy caravan, 1 bell tent, 1 hideout (stilted tent), 5 small tent pitches and a year-round holiday cottage. The communal campfire is at the centre of the site, as are the compost loos, jungle shower and field kitchen. This outdoor kitchen features gas cookers, straw-bale seats, cutlery, crockery, pots, pans, tea and coffee. Conventional loos (2W, 1M) and showers (1W, 1M) are also available in an outbuilding adjacent to the pub, and here you will also find a fridge/freezer, washing machine and microwave — all well tucked away so that the garden still feels wild and natural. There are a few groceries and free-range local meat for sale in the site's honesty shop.

✤ Nearby you can visit Framlingham Castle (01728 724189), an astonishingly fine 12th-century fortress with frequent child-friendly events. The coastal gems of Dunwich, Southwold and Aldeburgh are within easy striking distance, as is the world-famous RSPB bird reserve at Minsmere, with nature trails, hides and a visitor centre. The river Alde is explorable from Snape Maltings (01728 688303), where there are shops and restaurants and a concert hall that is home to the Aldeburgh Festival (01728 687110) every June.

✤ Alde Garden's onsite pub, The Sweffling White Horse Inn (East Anglia Pub of the Year 2015), is open 4 nights a week (Fri, Sat, Sun and Mon) plus Sunday lunchtimes, so you're often never more than stumbling distance away from a drink. They have an excellent (and ever-changing) selection of real ales — all from local breweries — and a small collection of organic fairtrade wines and speciality spirits, plus lots of other beverages. An off-licence service is available to Alde Garden guests (not just while the pub is open) via a stable door at the back of the pub.

✤ Open May–Oct.

✤ The Hideout £75 for 2 nights; bell tent £125 for 2 nights; gypsy caravan £170 for 2 nights; yurt £180 for 2 nights. Tents from £14 per night.

happy days
retro vacations

Moving out of London and living 'the dream' usually remains just that – a dream – for most of us. But for Kevin Armstrong, turning 40 and enduring a nasty motorbike accident turned the typical midlife crisis of 'fancy cars, fancy hairpieces and fast woman' into something more creative. His wife, Jenni, had fallen in love with beautiful, vintage Airstream caravans, and so on moving back to her childhood haunt, the couple threw themselves into the business of seeking out then doing up their own. Formerly based in East Dorset, 2015 saw the Happy Days team relocate to the tranquil outskirts of the peaceful Suffolk

market town of Saxmundham. Their newly acquired spot features ample room for their seven signature trailers and space for an additional four tents or visiting retro caravans/campers.

The 4–5-berth Airstreams are each decorated in a particular colour theme (Betsy – red; Gloria – burgundy and strawberry; Peggy – blue; Annie – flamingoes; Dee Dee – floral and gingham; Elsie – green vintage; and Netty – 70s retro) and feature original wood veneer interiors. Every attention to detail has been poured into the furnishings, with crochet blankets, quaint curtains and kitsch

cushions, while the retro feel of small items like the radio or strings of fairy lights and bunting add to the authentic feel of it all.

Outside, meanwhile, the new space has given room for adding a little extra flair to the proceedings. A polytunnel has been ingeniously converted into a cool social space – an all-season option for escaping the worst of the British weather – and a fantastic kids' play area with swings, slide and a giant trampoline has been crafted around the site's magnificently playful centrepiece: a 1950s French army truck that even the grown-ups will be clambering into!

The result is a site that really does seem to reflect Kevin and Jenni's dreams. Cooking up a feast on the gas cooker and eating it al fresco on the picnic table, you can't help but envy them. Fairy lights twinkle and the sun's light creates a farewell dance over the hedgerows opposite. Happy Days indeed.

Happy Days Retro Vacations, Wardspring Farm, Leiston Road, Saxmundham, Suffolk IP17 1TG
01728 603424 happydaysrv.co.uk

❋ Seven Airstreams, each with a firepit (wood available for £5), fridge/freezer, kettle, cooker, sink, toaster, DVD player, table and chairs, cooking utensils, WC for night-time use, games, torches, blanket plus other essential items including washing-up liquid, tea, coffee, salt and pepper. A new shower block features individual shower rooms and space for a family. There is a separate disabled access toilet and shower. Regular camping also available.

❋ Explore the seaside-shingle splendour of nearby Aldeburgh, as well as neighbouring Southwold and Thorpeness. Foodies flock to this part of the world for the region's various gastronomic gatherings, including the Aldeburgh Food and Drink Festival every September.

❋ The Bell at Sax (01728 602331) is mere minutes away and serves a menu of delicious, locally sourced dishes at reasonable prices; it also has a bustling bar. The fish don't come much fresher than those on offer at Sole Bay Fish Co. (01502 724241), right on the shore in Southwold harbour – the perfect setting for devouring plates of crab that have been landed fresh that morning.

❋ Open March–Nov. Changeover days Fri/Mon.

❋ From £220 for a 2-night weekend (Fri–Sun) stay, up to £730 for a week in high season.

ivy grange farm

London media world refugees Kim and Nick Hoare have created a real slice of rural bliss just outside the small Suffolk town of Halesworth, where five yurts form the nucleus of their thoughtfully planned glamping site. It's a place where attention has been paid to every sort of detail, and the enthusiasm and passion of the owners shines through at every turn.

The yurts themselves are beautifully furnished, with their own wood-burning stoves, comfy double beds and pull-out futons, and outside decking with a gas hob and firepit – great for taking in the big skies and glorious sunsets with a glass of wine each evening. There are cauldrons and cooking pots in the shed, and a wonderfully well-appointed open kitchen with a cob pizza oven for more ambitious (and more sociable) dining.

In addition to the three-acre field, there's a restored barn with tables and chairs, a lovely woodland (ie. outdoor) shower supplied by mains hot water, and you can pick the produce you need from the well-tended vegetable troughs around the barn – a board inside lists what's ready for harvest that day. It's all brilliantly done, and perfect for family groups or groups of families. Plus the location is great – right on a popular cycle route and just a few miles from the Suffolk coast at Southwold.

Ivy Grange Farm, Butts Road, Westhall, Halesworth, Suffolk IP19 8RN 07802 456087 ivygrangefarm.co.uk

❀ Five yurts in all. The smallest pair each sleep 3, a couple more can accommodate families of 4, while the largest sleeps 5. All the yurts have a rechargeable lantern, solar-powered fairy lights and their own wood-burning stoves; outside, each has a decking area with a BBQ and gas stove. There's a well-equipped outdoor kitchen and a pizza oven. The barn has charging-points for phones as well as table football, table tennis, games, books and Wi-Fi. Next door to the barn is a toilet and shower block, plus there's a solar-powered outdoor shower. Cookware is provided, as is a large basket of wood for the stove, while sheets and towels are an optional extra.

❀ The site is right on National Cycling Route 1, so it's perfect for exploring the flat, quiet roads nearby (there is a selection of bikes to borrow). You could also cycle to the Big Dog ferry nearby, a service which takes you to the unique Locks Inn pub just outside Geldeston (01508 518414). If you'd prefer stay put and drink in the peace of the camp, you could join one of the full moon walks the owners run every month.

❀ Westhall village is home to the Racehorse Inn (01502 575706), which is just over a mile away (a lovely quiet walk or bike ride) and does decent food. The White Hart at Blythburgh (01502 478217) and Queen's Head at Bramfield (01986 784214) are both worth a visit, as is St Peter's Brewery (01986 782322), a 15th-century moated manor house, just 5 miles away in 'The Saints', which has a shop, tours and a restaurant. Continuing the theme, if you are a brewery fan, do check out the brewery tours at Adnams in Southwold.

❀ Open mid March–Oct.

❀ Minimum stay 2 nights; low season prices start from £190 for 2 nights – look out for special offers and discounts for longer stays.

amber's bell tent camping

Mannington Hall is perhaps the quintessential English country house. A little outside the village of Itteringham, this stately Norfolk pile is straight out of the pages of *Country Life*, a 15th-century moated manor surrounded by spectacular gardens. With a dizzying array of plants and trees (over 1000 varieties of roses alone), they are a feast for the senses, with a walled garden, willow tunnel and even a secluded classical temple. Landscaped lakes in the sprawling grounds boast a water meadow whose vibrant flowers are a magnet for dragonflies, kingfishers and even the occasional otter. Oh, if only we could call this English country garden home!

Well, now we can. Fringed by an oak dell, Amber's bell tents occupy a three-acre field that overlooks the water meadows beyond Mannington's gardens. It's the realisation of a long-held dream of camping fan Amber and her family, who had the inspired idea of hooking up with Mannington's committed conservationist owners, Lord and Lady Walpole, to present a luxurious, low-impact bell tent site, starting in the gardens themselves and graduating to the larger field outside to enjoy more space. They've now been up and running for a few years, and it's fair to say Amber's is a place that is immensely popular. It's not hard to see why.

Airy and spacious, the five-metre, bunting-adorned tents are made of breathable natural cotton – the perfect antidote to stuffy polyester tents. Each tent is kitted out with cute vintage touches – the applecart tables-cum-storage boxes, a nice little nod to Norfolk's famous cider orchards. It's a proper glamper's scene, with double beds, wood-burning stoves, rugs, fairy lights, lanterns and a cool-box and cook kit. Yet for all the comforts, it's still about being outdoors. The tents even have an awning so you can spend the evening losing yourself to the light-pollution-free night sky. If you want a bit more privacy, and fancy being closer to the Hall itself, there is also a very comfortable shepherd's hut in the gardens proper.

The site has a sheltered kitchen, an eating and washing-up area, and a superb wood-fired sauna in the corner of the field. There is a tea room in the hall's gardens for afternoon snacks, and bespoke catering options can be arranged in advance. Amber's onsite honesty shop is also stocked with the essentials you'll need for a good campfire, including plenty of wood and fuel so you can toast those marshmallows deep into the wee hours.

Amber's Bell Tent Camping, Mannington Hall, Mannington, Norwich, Norfolk NR11 7BB
07580 072 861 ambersbelltents.co.uk

❀ Depending on time of year there are 4–7 tents, (each sleeping up to 5) in the main field, plus a shepherd's hut in its own meadow. Single and double beds are provided depending on your needs and all bedding is included (towels are an extra). A picnic table (per tent), combi BBQ/firepit, plus a kitchen box equipped with utensils and dishware. There's a washing-up tap in the field, plus loos and showers in the gardens about 200m away, and a sauna in the corner of the main field. Onsite honesty shop for fire essentials. Mannington Hall's gardens are yours to explore, plus there are nature packs for kids and badminton and boules on offer. Hire bikes can be dropped off at the site, plus Amber runs regular yoga retreats, wild camping weekends and bushcraft courses.

❀ With the Broads and the North Norfolk Coast practically on your doorstep, there's no shortage of great days out. The CanoeMan (0845 4969177) gives guided tours of these iconic waterways, while Holkham Bay is one of the latter's finest beaches. If you haven't had your fill of stately piles, Holkham Hall (01328 710806) and the National Trust-owned Felbrigg Hall (01263 837444) are within easy reach. You can also cycle the picturesque lanes surrounding Mannington itself.

❀ Mannington Hall has its own tea shop and campers can contact Helen from the tea room to pre-order hampers, cakes, campfire stews and other treats. There's also a tea room and village shop in Itteringham, a short walk across the fields. As for decent pubs, the Walpole Arms (01263 587258), a mile from the site, takes some beating. It's an 18th-century pub whose modern menu belie its traditional charms.

❀ Open late March–mid Autumn.

❀ Prices start at £85 a night.

deepdale

Come mid September, most people of sound mind put any thoughts of camping to rest. It's not just because the days start to turn colder but also because there aren't that many campsites that stay open once the leaves begin to curl and drop. Nudging the north Norfolk coastline, Deepdale Farm in Burnham Deepdale is a rare exception.

Some people believe there is no better time to visit Norfolk than autumn – the hedgerows are pregnant with blackberries and the county is a vision of russet-coloured forests and blush-coloured clouds – and Deepdale is a great place to come to if you do, with around 80 pitches and six tipis and yurts. These are not tipis awash with Indian silks and ethnic blankets, but they don't need to be. They are well maintained and equipped with a cast-iron chimenea for heat, including kindling and fuel for the fire, foldaway chairs, a BBQ and a lantern. Sleeping in the round, with the wind whispering softly above you, is enchantment enough.

There's often an enthusiastic programme of events at the farm, with everything from organised stargazing to cookery classes with local produce. But in any case there are diversions a-plenty in and around Burnham Deepdale. Kickstart the morning with a coffee at the café next door, and stock up on necessities at the nearby supermarket or onsite camping shop before hiring a bike or getting

on your walking boots. You are so near to the coastline here that an excursion to the water's edge is a must. Their insistence on post–10pm 'quiet time' means that loud and drunken tomfoolery is not tolerated – a good thing if you want to get out and about early.

Deepdale Backpackers and Campers, Burnham Deepdale, Norfolk PE31 8DD 01485 210256 deepdalebackpackers.co.uk

❄ There are 5 eco-friendly hot showers, 2 male toilets and 2 urinals, 3 female toilets, a unisex toilet block plus washing-up facilities. The water is heated by solar panels, with an oil burner back-up. No campfires.

❄ There is so much to do nearby that it's hard to know where to start. In one direction, to the east, Holkham Hall (01328 710227) is worth a visit, as is the famous expanse of Holkham Bay, with its giant pine-fringed beach. To the west, there is Holme Dunes Nature Reserve, while to the south, Burnham Market is probably Norfolk's poshest large village, with any number of places to eat and shop.

Just beyond there, yet another Burnham – Burnham Thorpe – is renowned as the birthplace of Admiral Lord Nelson, and has a fantastic small pub, the Lord Nelson (01328 738241), where they commemorate the great man with their own brand of spiced rum.

❄ Along with an onsite camping shop, the excellent Deepdale Café next door serves everything from quality English breakfasts to chunky homemade soup and evening meals in summer. The White Horse (01485 210262), a 5-minute walk west, is a buzzy gastropub serving local fish and shellfish, including cockles, mussels and oysters from the 'beds' at the bottom of the garden.

❄ Open all year.

❄ Tipis/yurts £40–£114/£50–£145 per night, depending on the time of year and the number of people.

wild luxury

They say that anyone can love the mountains, but it takes a soul to love the prairie. Well, Norfolk is that prairie, with its majestically flat landscape and never-ending skies. And by the end of your stay at Wild Luxury, you'll feel like a special soul indeed. Step into your lodge to be engulfed by the earthy scents of pine and cedar wood. From the floor to the furniture to the cabin bed, everything has been hobbitly hewn from natural materials. You even burn wood on your very own range. The seven lodges are completely off-grid. There's no electricity, and all the water is stored on site – in fact, for five months of the year there's nothing here but grass and badgers. So in many ways this is the wildest camping you could imagine, but there's nothing at all wild about having your own hot shower and flushing toilet. Dragging yourself away from your luxury lodge seems foolhardy, but it's worth it to discover that the whole of north Norfolk is right on your doorstep. Not only are there miles of beautiful coastline to explore, but endless inland diversions involving shire horses, country piles and adventure playgrounds, too. Back at camp, children are in their element – there are guinea pigs to cuddle, chickens to chase and making friends is a doddle. There's plenty of space in front of the lodges for kids to mingle, and evenings spent around the communal campfire are encouraged. So, just relax on the deck of your safari lodge, glass of wine in hand, and take a good long look at that breathtaking sunset in the endless expanse of the Norfolk sky… It's a bit good, isn't it?

Wild Luxury (The Hideaway), Hunstanton, Norfolk
01485 750850 wildluxury.co.uk

❀ Seven luxury safari lodges in a fenced-off field. Double bed, bunk beds and a cute double bed in a cupboard. All linen and towels are rentable. There is a wood-burning range in the kitchen and your day's allocation of firewood is supplied. There's also a double gas hob. All cookware, tableware and a cool-box are provided. Indulge in local sausages and bacon from the 'Wild Cooler' or stock up on essentials from the honesty pantry. You can also place orders for newspapers and fresh bread the day before. Bikes for all ages can be hired when booking — just remember to bring your own helmets. No cars are allowed in the field, except for unpacking/packing up.

❀ We have never seen such a comprehensive welcome pack as the one you're presented with here, so don't worry for a moment about being stuck for things to do, see or eat! There are nature walks from the site, and kids will love making friends with the guinea pigs and collecting eggs from the chickens. Beyond the site, the North Norfolk coast has plenty to tempt you, not least the beaches at Brancaster, Holme and Holkham, while a little way inland Pensthorpe Nature Reserve & Gardens (01328 851465) is home to numerous bird species and other wildlife.

❀ The Rose & Crown (01485 541382) in Snettisham is a proper local pub, but one which serves delicious food with a local slant. The award-winning Orange Tree (01485 512213) in Thornham is also a culinary force to be reckoned with. Don't let the X Factor-style flames outside put you off; the service is outstanding and the food local and innovative.

❀ Open late March–Oct.

❀ Serengeti lodges sleep up to 6, Zambezi lodges up to 10. Prices range from £269 for a 2-night weekend break in low season to £1495 for a week in the summer holidays. Dogs £5 each.

the chilterns view

The picture-perfect countryside and rural villages that pepper the Chiltern Hills have been tempting jaded Londoners out of the city for decades. And The Chilterns View is perhaps the perfect local spot from which to enjoy this beautiful region – not just for its position, which is ideal for exploring the surrounding countryside on foot; nor for the refined nature of the accommodation here. But also for its privacy, its peace and for the feeling that you have really escaped to somewhere special.

Cocooned in its own private world, The Chilterns View is home to five seriously luxurious glamping lodges situated in a dreamy garden-cum-meadow with a quiet pond behind your lodge and a south-facing veranda to the front. All have exceptional views of the surrounding countryside and, in summer, you can open up the floor-to-ceiling glass doors and let the outside in, toasting your holiday in the bubbling terrace hot tub (there's one outside each lodge) while sausages sizzle on the BBQ. When dusk falls into darkness, simply stoke the wood-burning stove and curl up with a good book (Agatha Christie was born in nearby Wallingford and *Midsomer Murders* was filmed nearby).

Without a TV in sight, this is a perfect place to escape the daily grind, although calling this 'glamping' is perhaps a bit of a stretch. Indeed, with a fully functioning kitchen, spacious wet room and speedy Wi-Fi, these are extremely well-equipped cabins. Their smallish size and natural surroundings still provide that camping feel, however, and glamping or not, it remains an eminently comfortable place for couples to hide away.

In any case the surroundings are ideal for shaking off everyday blues and enjoying some proper holiday time. It's a 10-minute walk into the picturesque village of Ewelme, which has a cosy village pub and an old church that you may recognise from the recent movie of *Les Misérables*, which was filmed here; while routes like the Chilterns Cycleway and Thames Path provide an easy way to explore the rest of the area. When you get back to base, the warmth of your Chilterns View abode is just what you need and affable host Rachel is welcoming, friendly and full of local knowledge. The dream, she tells us, was to share the beauty of the Ewelme Down Farm estate with others. With The Chilterns View we reckon she has done just that… and a whole lot more.

The Chilterns View, Ewelme Down Farm, Ewelme, Wallingford, Oxfordshire OX10 6PQ
01491 836353 thechilternsview.co.uk

❀ Five luxury lodges with room for 2 people – each fully equipped for self-catering and featuring a kitchenette, cosy living space, en suite shower room and a bedroom with a king-sized bed with linen, towels, bathrobes and toiletries, and with its own hot tub outside. There's also a supply of tea, coffee and milk, and each lodge has Wi-Fi and a docking station. The pond area has an open firepit and a large bespoke BBQ. Charcoal and wood for the lodges' BBQs and wood-burning stoves are available free of charge.

❀ The local area is perfect for walking and cycling, in particular the Ridgeway, Thames Path and Chilterns Cycleway, which offer easily navigable routes. By car, Oxford is the most popular day-trip, with plenty to keep you occupied, while in the opposite direction Henley-on-Thames is also well worth the journey. The nearby village of Ewelme is recognised for its historic church and graveyard, along with its unique watercress beds (01494 771250).

❀ There are lots of pubs within walking distance. The Shepherd's Hut (01491 836636) in Ewelme has food and a wonderfully friendly atmosphere. Home Sweet Home in Wallingford (01491 838249) is another old joint with a cosy feel and good food. The Lord Nelson (01491 612497) in Brightwell Baldwin is a traditional old pub serving excellent food. The King William IV in Ipsden (01491 681845) is the busiest of the lot but has a lovely setting and a fantastic menu.

❀ Open all year.

❀ £165 per night Sun–Thurs based on a minimum 2-night stay (otherwise £250); £195 per night Fri and Sat based on a minimum 2-night stay. No 1-night stays Fri and Sun.

cotswolds camping

The historic county of Warwickshire is geographically and culturally (as birthplace of the Bard) at the heart of England, boasting some of the country's most quintessentially English towns and villages. Unfortunately, for enthusiasts of the very British pastime of camping, it has often tended to offer much ado about nothing – until now. Because the village of Whichford harbours one of the county's best-kept camping secrets, a mash-up of the medieval, Middle-Eastern and mystical that is unlikely to stay a secret for too long.

The six-acre site is situated in the grounds of a Norman castle, the legacy of which is a splendid water-filled moat. Local mystics have it that Holycombe was a sacred Neolithic site, evidenced by six converging ley-lines, so it

would have been a shame not to add a stone circle or two. The irony is that this rich heritage lay beneath a scrapyard until Sally and Andy Birtwell built their eco-home and holistic retreat here, along with an alternative camping site that's perfect for purists and – with a yurt, airstream, treehouse, gypsy caravan and bell tents – part-timers too.

Holycombe adjoins Whichford Wood, a wildlife-filled SSSI. It's also handily located a short walk from a classic Cotswold pub, so after a long ramble or a pint you can light a campfire as dusk settles on the valley, and banter long into the night about whether ley-lines really do exist, or ponder what might be lurking at the bottom of that mysterious moat.

Cotswolds Camping, Holycombe, Whichford Castle Moat, Whichford, Shipston-on-Stour, Warwickshire CV36 5PH 01608 684239 cotswoldscamping.com

❀ Forty camping pitches, 2 bell tents, a treehouse, airstream caravan, gypsy wagon and a yurt. Campfires are allowed, and wood can be bought on site. Bell tents are equipped with rugs, eco-lanterns and futon-style beds. The tree house has its own compost loo and washing-up station. The kitchen cabin has a fridge, sink, electric cooker and seating. There are 2 hot electric showers and 3 loos plus a heated shower and loo exclusive to glampers. No children under 12 years of age and no groups permitted (the focus here is on peace and quiet!).

❀ Holycombe adjoins Whichford Wood, where you might see Muntjac deer, polecats, kingfishers and more. Continue exploring the mystical at the Rollright Stones, 3 miles up the A3400. Or take home a handmade terracotta memento from Whichford Pottery (01608 684416) – also home to the excellent Straw Kitchen.

❀ The Norman Knight pub is a half-mile walk away (01608 684621) for real ales, flagstone floors, exposed timbers and gastropub grub. Wyatts Farm Shop (01608 684835), near Greater Rollright, has a good selection of local produce and there's a village shop in Long Compton.

❀ Open all year but bell tents April–Oct only.

❀ Glamping accommodation all costs from £65 per night – 2-night minimum stay on weekends and bank holidays.

the dome garden

Ten geodesic domes have sprung up in the garden of a former dilapidated Forestry Commission lodge, which itself is now an ultra-modern wooden home-cum-breakfast-bar-hangout. And, as the years go by, like the ancient trees in the forest surrounding the garden, this place is blooming into something magnificent. Owner Jonny and his family were dedicated tipi-campers until one winter they made a snow dome that could sleep 10 people. When it melted, they decided to invest in some permanent structures, and the Dome Garden was born.

The garden already has a sociable vibe, with kids making friends on the rope swings and small zip-wires, or running out into the forest. The ever-growing willow tunnels and clever landscape gardening allow plenty of space for privacy, but by night-time, once the pizza oven is lit and everyone's making their own creations, even the most hermit-like campers will find it hard not to join in.

Yes, this is glamping on a grand scale. But if you're no fan of the outdoors and open fires, do not apply. Wood is used for cooking or heating, from simple stick-heaters to the garden's central firepit. There are so many innovative yet simple touches here that you'll be hard-pushed to find anywhere else like it. Lime-green AstroTurf carpets your dome, kids sleep in hanging pods and there's an ambient light to see what colour your dome glows after dark. Kevin McCloud would indeed call it a work of grand design.

The Dome Garden, Mile End, Coleford, Gloucestershire GL16 7EN 07974 685818 domegarden.co.uk

---

❄ Eleven domes (sleeping 2–9 people; bedding provided) each with a wood-burning stove. En suite wet rooms have a shower, a flushing loo and a washbasin; the water is heated when you light a tiny wood boiler. One dome has full disabled facilities. Each dome has its own 'forest kitchen' and a stick-powered stove for outdoor cooking and a natural food safe. There is a communal outdoor washing-up area and a dedicated 'Babyshack' with everything parents need to help look after tiny tots. At night the communal firepit provides a great focal point.

❄ Rope swings a-plenty, a wobbly tyre wall connected to a zip wire and chickens to feed will all keep the little ones busy. The Forest of Dean is on your doorstep, explorable via a 12-mile circular Family cycle trail and a 7-mile off-road route that runs past the garden gate. The Forestry Commission's Beechenhurst Lodge (01594 833057) has a large outdoor adventure playground for young kids and is the starting point for the free Sculpture Trail.

❄ The Dome Garden has its own bar and runs a hugely popular pizza night twice a week. You can eat Dome Garden homecooked breakfasts if you don't want to make your own, or take advantage of an increasing range of wood-fired food, from 'Perfect Pork' to 'Best Beef Ever'. Coleford has 2 butchers selling locally sourced meat, and the Crusty Loaf bakery (01594 832360) makes a delicious range of breads, including ancient recipes twice a week.

❄ Open most of the year (out of season by arrangement).

❄ A Simple Dome for 4 adults or 5 people (including kids) costs from £345 for 4 midweek nights in low season to £995 for a week in high season.

out to grass

More laid-back than a sun lounger and more chilled-out than a pack of frozen peas, Out To Grass is a camping and glamping site with a perfectly appropriate name. Just as the winter-born calves bound from their sheds in May and clumsy-legged foals spring from their stables after quiet months inside, this green and spacious place is a spot for summertime crowds to truly escape. Kids run free – think grass stains and muddy patches as if straight off a washing detergent advert – and adults kick back, enjoying an evening pint in the site's very own bar. We don't gnaw, we don't graze, we don't nibble on the grass, but all the same, you'll be as happy here as any animal on earth.

Tucked away in a quiet corner of Worcestershire, in the rolling fringes of the Malvern Hills, Out To Grass is a do-as-you-please campsite with an effortlessly cool ethos and a relaxed atmosphere. And, best of all for aspirant glampers, it has a series of luxurious bell pods designed specifically for the site, furnished with beds (and bedding), rugs, proper chairs and kitchen equipment. The site's washing facilities are relatively basic, with three toilets and two showers, but they're clean and perfectly adequate, while a huge geodesic dome houses a communal covered area with a pool table, games and sofas – plus there's a campsite bar and café. The general feel is a bit like a summer festival, with regular night-time music – though usually at a low enough level that when you slip off to bed you're completely undisturbed – and plenty of campfires. On most Fridays there is even a communal fireplace blazing, with camp stews cooked up for everyone, followed by marshmallows and hot chocolate.

If you can drag yourself away from the site, there's plenty to discover in the countryside around. The Malvern Hills are riddled with excellent footpaths and their namesake town is peppered with independent shops and pleasant little cafés. The area was also the home of composer Edward Elgar and you can visit his birthplace just outside the the nearby county town of Worcester, less than half an hour away from the site.

Worcester itself makes for a good day out, with a liberal dollop of half-timbered Tudor buildings and regal Georgian homes intermingled with more stark modern structures. However, the most timeless feature of the place is the River Severn, flowing along the city's western edge and past the mighty cathedral – which is also a must-visit. The town has a wonderfully compact and walkable centre and offers the perfect urban day-trip. All the better as a contrast before you make the short journey back to the site to be put back Out To Grass.

Out To Grass, Woodend Farm, Bromyard Road, Cradley, Malvern, Worcestershire WR13 5JW
01886 880099 outtograss.com

❀ Four bell pods, 3 proper toilets and 1 portable-style toilet, 2 showers, a kitchen area, plus a bar, shop and café. There is a pool table for anyone to use and onsite fun and games include walks through the woods, treasure hunts and ghostly evening tales. Campfires permitted.

❀ Come in spring to enjoy the best of the bluebells in the Malvern Hills AONB (01684 560616) and the woodland that neighbours the campsite, where there are a few great walking trails to discover. The local spa town of Malvern is worth a visit – try the Malvern Splash Leisure Centre (01684 893423) on rainy days – and for a little culture and history, the National Trust-owned Brockhampton Estate (01885 482077), with its 14th-century manor house and vast grounds. It's just 12 miles to the county town of Worcester, notable for its pleasant old centre and grand cathedral (01905 732900). Just outside Worcester, visit the birthplace of iconic English composer Edward Elgar, now a considerable museum to the man and his work.

❀ There is an onsite bar and café that serves breakfasts, coffee and teas as well as some light bites. The nearest pub, a couple of miles away at Stiffords Bridge, is the Red Lion Inn (01886 880318), which does food, although the best place to eat and drink is tucked away in Bishops Frome 3 miles away – the ivy-covered Green Dragon Inn (01885 490607), a low-beamed country pub that serves regularly changing cask ales and good, homecooked pub grub. In Malvern try the Blue Bird Tea Room (01684 575031).

❀ Open early May–early Oct.

❀ Bell pods £80 for 1 night, £150 for 2 nights, £175 for 3 nights and a refundable deposit of £80 prior to arrival. Two-night minimum in the pods at weekends.

drover's rest

There are two types of middle-of-nowhere. The first is a leafy, inaccessible backwater. The second is somewhere that's easy to get to, but once you arrive there's not much there, save for the birds and the bees and a pleasant country breeze. Far off the beaten track, Drover's Rest is just such a place and makes for a truly idyllic glamping destination. With easy access to Hay-on-Wye and the Brecon Beacons, yet retaining its own secluded space in the Herefordshire countryside, it's still a working farm that has only relatively recently begun converting its outbuildings into cosy, modern cottages. However, it's the five brand-new safari tents that have been added

that tickled our taste buds, for letting the outside in and providing a real on-the-farm experience.

The creamy canvas cottages really thrust guests into the outdoors, set as they are in a grassy meadow overlooking pastures dotted with sheep. Outdoor furniture lets you prop yourself up on the deck and breathe in the fresh country air as you admire the scenery, while inside, the glamping-style accommodation pushes the boundaries of where exactly camping ends and hotel living begins. Rooms (divided by the inner canvas lining) separate two sleeping areas from an open-plan living space, which comes complete with a wood-burning stove, fridge, gas stove and pretty much all the kitchen equipment you could need – though, if you want a more rustic vibe, there's a three-legged pot outside for cooking over the campfire.

The farm's hayloft is now a chill-out barn with an honesty shop, Wi-Fi and giant TV, but the real appeal of the site is to be among the simple rusticity of general farming life that's been plodding along here for centuries. It's a thoroughly hands-on place and perfect for kids, with all sorts of things to get involved in, from collecting eggs and herding sheep to milking goats or churning cheese. Indeed, those wanting a perfect family experience can let little ones pick apples before pressing them for cider and finally letting the adults perform that all-important tasting! Off site, step back into reality (yes, it's out there) and zip down the road to Hay-on-Wye, an attractive riverside town where winding streets are lined with old stone buildings. For every stone you're likely to find a different book – it seems to be all the place exists for – but between the bookshops there are also some top-quality eateries tucked away. Beyond Hay, the trails and cycle routes of the Brecon Beacons beckon – a middle-of-nowhere place that perfectly complements the middle-of-everything feel of this carefree rural campsite.

Drovers Rest, Llanycoed Farm, Off Watery Lane, Hay-on-Wye, Herefordshire HR3 6AG
01497 831215 droversrest.co.uk

❋ Five canvas cottages on decks, keeping them flat and making the most of the views. Each has 2 bedrooms with proper beds (linen and duvets included), an open-plan lounge, kitchen and dining area with a wood-burning stove, gas stove, fridge and outdoor furniture on the deck. Each has its own bathroom with underfloor heating, shower and loo. All have electricity and water, with laundry available if required. Campers have access to a communal barn, which has Wi-Fi, Sky TV, a games console, books, games and a farm shop with a small café-bar for cake and cocktails! Guests are encouraged to get involved in farm life, such as collecting the eggs, feeding the animals and even making cheese.
❋ The local village of Hay-on-Wye is rightfully famous for its annual literary festival and is a treasure trove for antiques and interesting boutiquey shops (see p.129). Its riverside location and proximity to the Brecon Beacons also makes it a haven for outdoor types.
❋ By day, along with its produce for sale, the onsite farm shop has a pleasant café. By night it has a communal, almost pub-ish feel, serving dinner three nights a week, including a BBQ night with the farm's own meats. Hay-on-Wye offers stiff competition, with lots of decent places to eat, including the Blue Boar (01497 820884), which is good for real ales and wet-weather fires and serves excellent food, and the Granary (01497 820790), an unpretentious café-bistro with good veggie options.
❋ Open Easter–end Oct.
❋ From £695–£895 per week; £417–£595 for a short break (Mon–Fri, or Fri–Mon).

wye glamping

Tucked away on a lush, arable farm, with awe-inspiring views of the Black Mountains and Brecon Beacons, lies eco-friendly Wye Glamping. The site's ethos is simple: relax and cosy up with Mother Nature in true comfort and style. Take a stroll through the rolling countryside, splash in the onsite stream, or simply settle down with a good book and take in the beautiful green expanse of your mountain surroundings. And isn't that exactly how glamping should be?

Guests have the choice of two kinds of accommodation. Firstly, tucked away along a hedgerow is an impressive 18-ft yurt. Sitting slightly raised atop pristine decking, this fully furnished abode provides glorious, panoramic views of the field and beyond. Given the lack of light pollution, the yurt is perfect for a spot of stargazing, and on a clear Brecon night the sky illuminates impressively. The site also has four bell tents. Set alongside the nearby meandering river, each dwelling is located far enough apart to create a sense of seclusion, yet close enough for groups who wish to camp together.

Facilities at Wye Glamping are ample to say the least. Both the yurt and each of the bells has their own adjacent kitchen hut, which comes fully loaded with a gas stove, grill, pots, pans, cutlery, crockery and everything else you could possibly need. At the entrance to the 'Glamping Field' you'll find a luxurious washblock with a hot shower, a bath and a proper flushing loo. Each pitch also comes with a private compost loo – extremely handy for those midnight dashes!

Wye Glamping couldn't be better located to explore the gorgeous, undulating Brecon Beacons National Park. Waterfalls? Rolling fields? Charming Welsh towns? They're all here. From the peaks of Cribyn mountain to the depths of its limestone caves, there's plenty to see and do in this stunner of a national park. And being so close to all the action, Wye Glamping is the ideal base from which to go and explore it all.

Wye Glamping, The Old Estate Yard, Felindre, Brecon, Powys LD3 0SU 07974 000421 wyeglamping.co.uk

❀ One yurt and 4 bell tents (each on raised wooden decks) with gravel paths leading to each pitch. Accommodation comes fully furnished with a double bed, linen, reed matting on the floor, and 2 single futons in the bells (3 in the yurt), and rugs, cushions, blankets and pillows. Shared shower facilities (including a shower room, bath room, and flushing loo); each pitch also has its own compost loo. Each accommodation has a fully equipped private kitchen with double-burner grill, cool-box, cool packs, utensils, crockery and pots. Basics such as tea, coffee, sugar, milk, oil, clingfilm and foil are provided. Picnic bench, deck chairs, firepit/BBQ at each pitch and wood-burning stove inside (bag of wood, kindling and firelighters provided, with more available on site).

❀ The local market town of Hay-on-Wye (or *Y Gelli Gandryll* in Welsh) is often described as 'the town of books', and with good cause! Books really are everywhere; the cinema's a bookshop, the fire station's a bookshop, the castle's a bookshop, even the alleyways are bookshops. And if you plan your visit in May you'll catch the annual Festival of Literature (01497 822629).

❀ Along with excellent eateries there are several independent delis, greengrocers, butchers and bakers in Hay-on-Wye at which to pick up fresh local produce. The closest supermarket is 2 miles away. The charming Three Horseshoes (01497 847304) is a lovely country pub that is conveniently located at the campsite's entrance and does good food.

❀ Open Easter–Autumn half-term.

❀ Prices based on a 3-night weekend or 4-night midweek stay are £275–£345 for a bell tent, £325–£425 for a yurt.

cosy under canvas

Cosy Under Canvas, Dolbedwyn, Newchurch, Kington, Powys HR5 3QQ 01497 851603
cosyundercanvas.co.uk

❉ Seven geodesic domes each sleep up to 4 people (the larger domes have room for 2 extra kids) and contain a double or king-sized bed and 2 futon beds with memory foam mattresses. Inside, you'll find Welsh blankets, throws, a wooden storage box, candles, and cotton bedding. There's a chimenea on the decking and a private firepit each. There's also a communal kitchen and tripod stands. Throw in a 'cosy corner' complete with games and activities, private wood-fired hot tubs (in the larger domes only), private compost loos, recycling facilities, hammocks, ice packs, cool-boxes and dry storage containers, and you're all sorted!

❉ The site edges the Brecon Beacons (01874 624437), so any route you choose to take will be a walker's paradise. Beyond its boundary, Offa's Dyke Path forms the border between England and Wales. For something more mellow, try exploring nearby Hay-on-Wye (see p.129).

❉ Try the Roast Ox (01497 851398) in Painscastle for a great-value pub meal.

❉ Open April—mid Oct.

❉ Cosy domes for up to 2 people cost from £175 for a midweek break in low season to £695 for a week in peak season. Spacious domes cost £295 midweek in low season to £885 for a full week in peak season.

Twisting and turning along the winding country lanes, surrounded by undulating green and yellow fields deep in the heart of the Welsh/English Borders, it's almost impossible not to get childishly giddy about the treats that await you at Cosy Under Canvas. As you slowly roll into the car park, offload your bags into the wheelbarrow kindly provided for you, and walk along the wooden manmade pathway across a sea of wildflower wetland, it quickly becomes apparent that when it comes to glamping, you can never underestimate a woman's touch.

Owner Emma has been running Cosy Under Canvas for seven years now, and oh, does her experience resonate throughout the site! From the little welcome boards with your names written in chalk, to the homemade cakes left out for your arrival.

The site is made up of seven pitches, all spread out among a small private woodland, and cleverly hidden from each other by the trees. There are five spacious and cosy geodesic dome tents – Hazel, Rowan, Holly, Oak and Beech; and two beautifully furnished smaller domes, Ash and Willow. All the pitches come with their own private firepit, recycled gas bottle chimenea, compost loo, indoor wood-burning stove, sheepskin rugs, double or king-size beds, kindling, beanbags, lanterns

and tea lights. The larger domes all come with their own private wood-fired outdoor hot tubs, and some have views overlooking the stunning surrounding wildflower wetlands. There's a 'cosy corner', which is filled with board games and activities for kids and a large communal sheltered kitchen, which comes equipped with everything you could possibly need for cooking up a storm over a campfire, from tripods, skillets and pots and pans to chopping boards, cool-boxes and even a brand new pizza oven. There's also fresh drinking water and a handful of gas stoves in case the rain tries to put a dampener on things. The two communal showers are heated by the large wood-fired Aga in the kitchen – a nice communal touch, as it relies on everyone chucking in a log from time to time to make sure the water stays hot. It's no real wonder, then, that Cosy Under Canvas is also the proud owner of a much coveted gold Green Tourism Award.

Add together all of these seemingly endless well-thought-out touches and you can easily see why this is a woodland retreat like no other. It's a series of camping oxymorons: rugged, earthy daintiness; muddy, organised plots; rustic, frilly communal areas; and axes lying next to hammocks. The kids will never want to get out of the hot tub, and couples will only want to cosy up with each other next to the fire and stare up at the dark starry night sky above them. Should you decide to venture out of cosy-camping central, then you will no doubt stumble into the literary haven of Hay-on-Wye – the host town for the annual Literary Festival, which is awash with excellent book shops. There are plenty of organic delis, antique stalls and bric-a-brac gems to keep you occupied for a full day. But if you prefer the more outdoorsy side of living, Hay-on-Wye also happens to be situated within the 520 square miles of the Brecon Beacons National Park. That's 520 square miles of uninterrupted, unspoiled, and truly outstanding natural beauty. And yes, this is yet another excellent reason to choose to stay at Cosy Under Canvas.

powys pods

Powys Pods try to avoid the term 'glamping', because they still very much class themselves as a camping site – albeit a campsite with some very wooden-looking tents. "We cater to the muddy boots brigade", owner Jess tells us. "You need to bring everything that you would for camping, but you can leave the tent at home".

It may sound unusual, but it's a simple idea and one that she pulls off to perfection. Comprised of just three wooden pods, each with electricity and a heater, the site's accommodation is simple yet more than comfortably adequate. Unlike some bells-and-whistles glamping sites, Powys Pods hasn't clogged every space with spangled chandeliers and layers of fancy bedding, but instead offers the convenience of simple, sturdy accommodation that allows you to have a more traditional camping break without any weather worries. Outside, there's room to sit in the sun and while away the hours while the essential joys of stargazing and late-night campfires are still very much encouraged. It really is camping without the peg-pushing, pole-snapping, nylon-fighting hasssle.

On a tiered slope in rural Radnorshire, the pods are located on semi-organic Grug Farm, which is home to 200 sheep and half a dozen Welsh Black cows that graze either side of the winding, local lanes. Two of the three units are in the lower camping area – where separate wooden buildings with toilets and modern, power showers can also be found – while the third pod is hidden away further up the slope, in a field of its own. The winning factor for all three is undoubtedly the view. In the foreground, below your camping space, a block of trees spreads throughout the valley bottom, while behind it, hills climb up gently towards the sky. The higher pod, meanwhile, overlooks a stretch of open fields, the Black Mountains visible in the distance on a clear day.

In the way all good views do, it can't help but catch your attention. No sooner have you sat yourself down and you're drawing a line with your finger across the nearest hillside. Jess will help to answer all your questions and can direct you to nearby Offa's Dyke footpath, though simply taking off to explore will quickly reveal a host of local treasures. An easy 20-minute car journey brings you to famous Hay-on-Wye, its quirky independent book and antique shops giving it an enjoyable buzz that lasts well beyond the annual Hay Festival.

Powys Pods, Grug Farm, Bryngwyn, Kington, Powys HR5 3QN 01497 851666
powyspods.co.uk

❀ Just 3 pods: Bryn-Gwyn (sleeps up to 5 adults), Allt Dderw (sleeps up to 2 adults and 2 small children), and Ardwyn (sleeps 2 adults and 1 infant). Tents sometimes permitted as part of pod booking. 2 luxury showers and 3 toilets in separate pod units, along with a drying room with space to hang clothes. The pods all have electricity, with sockets for charging essentials, and a small oil-filled radiator/fan heater adds to the cosy feeling. One of the pods (Ardwyn) also has built-in beds with mattresses and storage underneath, which can either be set as 2 single beds or converted into a double. The site has a fantastic lawn area (subject to tents) for playing games, and there is a firepit, undercover seating and BBQ area.

❀ Less than a mile from the site, Bryngwyn Riding Centre can saddle you up (both beginners and the experienced) for a pony trek across the Welsh countryside. Options vary from short half-hour routes for kids to whole-day hacks for committed grown-ups. The local, heather-clad hills are covered in bridleways and riding is a fantastic way to cover the ground. Also popular is a drive to the River Wye, where you can hire canoes (07414 935965) and drift your way down stream. For something a little more sedate, Hay-on-Wye (see p.129) has a wealth of good independent shops and places to eat.

❀ The nearest pub is the Roast Ox (01497 851398) at Painscastle (4 miles away), which serves good food and real ales; there's also a good bar and restaurant at Rhosgoch Golf Club, 3 miles away (01497 851251).

❀ Open March–Oct.

❀ Pods sleep 2–5 people and cost £35–£45 per night.

redwood valley

As any good nursery school teacher will tell you, the easiest way to tell the age of a tree is to keep walking until you can put your hands on your knees, peer back, upside down, through your legs and see the very top of the branches in the distance. The number of paces you have to walk is the amount of years that tree has grown. It's a crude method, but few things will delight you more than seeing a forest full of kiddies bobbing up and down and ducking their heads between their legs like a field of oversized chickens. At Redwood Valley, they'd have to walk a long, long way.

Deep in the wilds of the Welsh border, this secluded haven is home to such vast trees that you can't help but be enthralled by them. At its heart is the giant redwood that gives this campsite its name, a tall grandfather of the forest, with its distinctive auburn bark. Even the site's rope-swing has to do that bit extra to fit in – the rope from branch to swing is about 20ft long! Snuggled among it all, Redwood Valley is a site with a clear affinity with its surroundings. With just two yurts and a woodland cabin, effortlessly blended in among the forest backdrop, the place is quiet, unobtrusive and effortlessly charming. The more curvaceously roofed of the two yurts (built in the Turkmen style) has wonderful

steam-bent wooden latticework inside and simple yet extremely comfortable furnishings. The second, Mongolian-style structure has a little more flair than its partner; the door and interior woodwork are hand-painted in a decorative, traditional style, and extra furnishings, like fairy lights, add to the magical feel. The separate, cosy cabin is perched high on the slope overlooking the brook. Lovingly crafted from timber from the valley, it seems to melt from view, offering complete privacy. The cabin is raised on stilts and, from its balcony, you feel almost a part of the canopy, alone among the birds.

All three structures benefit from a snug wood-burning stove inside and a firepit-cum-BBQ outside. Campfire cooking, though, is a primitive choice in comparison to the wooden kitchen lodge, which has an almost Scandinavian feel. Set into a bank with trees all around, it features fridges, hobs and everything you'd expect of most holiday-home kitchens, transplanted to this breathtakingly wild setting – a truly special place in which to prepare your supper. The same building houses an excellent gas-powered shower, while a long, hand-crafted table allows for a leisurely feast as the sun disappears beneath the tree tops.

Redwood Valley, Boultibrooke House, Norton Road, Presteigne, Powys LD8 2EU 01544 598050 redwood-valley.co.uk

❋ Cabin (sleeping up to 4) with private composting toilet and 2 yurts (sleeping up to 5 each). Both feature a king-sized bed (bedding included), a single and double futon, bedside lights, wind-up lanterns and a wood-burning stove. Outside, each yurt has a spring water tap, BBQ and firepit, table and stools, while the communal woodland kitchen is equipped with 2 fridges, gas hobs, microwave, toaster, utensils, cutlery and crockery – plus tea, coffee, sugar, condiments and herbs. There is a long table on which to eat or play games provided. Next to the kitchen is an excellent gas-heated shower (complimentary toiletries) and a composting toilet.

❋ Under a mile from Redwood Valley, Presteigne is a thriving town with a wine bar, 4 pubs and an eclectic array of independent shops and eateries. For something a little more in keeping with the campsite setting, there's a fantastic farm park and owl sanctuary (01544 231109) just a few miles away. The campsite is located in the heart of a dark sky reserve and if you want to do more than the stargazing on site, there's an observatory (01547 520247) located just up the road in Knighton – bring a telescope if you're keen!

❋ Presteigne has an excellent greengrocer and fishmonger, a deli selling freshly baked bread, a local butcher, a wine shop and two small supermarkets. Of the town's pubs, there is the simple Farmers Inn (01544 267389), the grander Radnorshire Arms (01544 267406) and the convivial Royal Oak (01544 260842), plus the new Duck's Nest (01544 598090) – an excellent choice.

❋ Open April–Oct.

❋ Yurts £100–£150 per night. Price includes firewood.

ty cefn tregib

Ty Cefn Tregib, Ffairfach, Llandeilo, Carmarthenshire SA19 6TD 01558 823830 tregib.co.uk

❋ Two yurts and a vintage American Airstream, all with everything you need, including electricity, a huge double bed (can be divided into 2 singles), sofa, table and chairs, firewood, showers and a side-wagon with a power point. Each unit has its very own kitchen and shower room facility. Optional continental breakfast basket for your first morning (£10 per couple); just ask when you book.

❋ Sitting proudly above the River Towy, there can't be many towns in Wales more attractive than Llandeilo. This charming place has a wealth of historic monuments, including the magical Dinefwr Castle (01558 824512) and the unique Roman Gold Mines at Dolaucothi (01558 650177).

❋ Llandeilo has a good selection of eateries, from the Olive Branch Delicatessen (01558 823030), which offers a wide range of refined local produce, to the excellent Angel (01558 822765), which is probably the town's best restaurant.

❋ Open Easter–Autumn half-term.

❋ Yurt/Airstream prices range from £250–£300 for a Fri–Mon or Mon–Fri stay, with discounts for longer periods. Each unit accommodates 2 people.

Ty Cefn Tregib is a true family affair. Indeed, the whole concept first started when John and Mary Evans' children first moved out, leaving spare bedrooms for starting their own homely B&B. And now, more than two decades on, the place has come full circle, with daughter Cass doing much of the hosting, while her parents tend the garden and potter around the site. It was Cass, too, who bought the classic American Airstream, a new feature for the 10-acre plot that's nestled in its own private woodland glade. This supremely cool caravan has been refurbished inside and out, complete with a modern kitchen, DVD television and outdoor decking, and joins the site's two longer-standing features – a pair of beautiful yurts, which were first introduced by Mary back in 2006.

The B&B-style approach extends to all these various hideouts. The motto of the owners is simple – "just get here"; there's no need to bring bedding, towels, torches, or even bed sheets as all guests are fully taken care of in a way only Ty Cefn Tregib knows how. Sometimes little things can make a big difference. For example, Mary replaces the handmade outer-covers of the yurts every two seasons, keeping the accommodation looking fresh and unspoiled all year round.

Both yurts are in prime areas of the land – the Mongolian yurt has a fabulous view of the Towy River valley and the other, oriental styled Pagoda yurt, is tucked close to a cascading waterfall. Inside, if you look closely enough, you'll discover artistic touches that help create a beautiful ambience. Take, for instance, the colourfully painted bedstead in the former, or the authentic Japanese Noren door hangings that adorn the Pagoda walls.

Ty Cefn Tregib's location is also a winner. At the foot of the Brecon Beacons, it acts as a seasonal base for all things outdoors, in particular for world-class mountain biking, with some of the best trails right on your doorstep. The busy local village of Ffairfach is only a short walk away, while the lovely market town of Llandeilo is within a mile and has bookshops, cafés, galleries, and delis to keep you busy for a few days.

cwm ty coed

Tucked away down a sleepy country lane, glampsite Cwm Ty Coed (literally 'Wood House Valley') can be found in one of Carmarthenshire's more secluded pockets, just off the A48. Once you have found it, you will be entranced by the panoramic views of rolling countryside and magical woodlands at this charming 30-acre smallholding. It's little wonder that Carmarthen has been named 'The Garden of Wales'.

First up, accommodation. The adjectives 'cosy', 'warm' and 'comfortable' fail to do justice to the site's yurt, two tipis and five bell tents. Guests will feel like the proverbial cat that got the cream on discovering the large beds, candle lanterns and private kitchen. Outside, there's your own firebowl, wood–burning stove and BBQ; it's the perfect setting in which to cook up that tasty Welsh produce.

The nearby hills and coastline offer hours of exploration. Pembrey Country Park, with miles of deserted beach, can be reached within 15 minutes by car, and to the east are the breathtaking bays and subterranean coves of Gower. Carmarthen itself is steeped in history, the oldest town in Wales and the birthplace of everyone's favourite Arthurian wizard, Merlin. More recent history could draw you to the picturesque village of Laugharne and Dylan Thomas's house, with its evocative views across the Three Rivers estuary.

Back at Cwm Ty Coed, owners Jon and Sarah not only want guests to enjoy the comforts of five-star glamping but also to experience a taste of traditional, rural camping, with sing–a–longs by roaring campfires and magical nights spent gazing up at the starry Welsh skies.

Cwm Ty Coed , The Valley, Carmarthenshire SA31 2LS
07463 389476 / 01267 233884 cwmtycoed.co.uk

❄ Five bell tents, 2 tipis and a yurt, all fully furnished with wooden floors, lanterns, solar lighting and proper beds with cosy bedding and blankets. Tipis each have a large central chiminea and the yurt and bell tents each have a wood-burning stove. Each pitch comes with private kitchen fully equipped for camp cooking and dining, with outdoor firepit, BBQ, picnic bench and deck chairs. Shared facilities include gas-powered showers in the camping fields and compost toilets. There is a large, communal wood cabin with wood-burning stove, sofas, kitchen, table tennis, games and books as well as mains electricity for charging phones, etc. Woodland walks are possible from the site and the field is surrounded by swings, slides and even a zip-wire. An outdoor cinema in the woods can be enjoyed with straw-bale sofas around a large firepit. Firewood is supplied for all fires. There are plenty of animals to see, and you can collect eggs from the hens and meet the friendly donkeys, Misty and Lily.

❄ Kids can do their own weaving at the free National Woollen Museum (02920 573070), or visit the splendid National Botanic Gardens (01558 668768). Take a trip to the ancient standing stones of Myndd Llangyndeyrn, a SSSI that attracts an abundance of rare birds and uncommon invertebrates.

❄ Carmarthen Market (01267 228841) sells local cheeses and Carmarthen ham, a serious local rival to the Parma variety. You can also pick up your sausages and burgers here for that evening BBQ. There are a couple of decent pubs in nearby Pontyberem – the New Inn (01269 871152), with good pub food and a range of ales, and the Smiths Arms (01269 842213), which is a bit closer to the site in Foelgastell.

❄ Open mid March–end Sept.

❄ Tipis £80/£90 per night (low/high season), bell tents £70/£80 per night, yurt £95/£110 per night. Extra tent £10 per night. Discounts available for weekly stays.

the ceridwen centre

To call The Ceridwen Centre a campsite is like saying Da Vinci was a bit handy with a paintbrush. For this purpose-built hillside hideaway is as adept at hosting workshops, retreats, courses and weddings as it is at hosting your glamping getaway. Nestled within 40 acres of lush (an adjective the locals are fond of) West Wales farmland, Ceridwen lies in the fabled Teifi Valley, which straddles Ceredigion and Carmarthenshire. Helmed by helpful host Simone, the site wears its green credentials proudly. There's a range of ingenious environmental features all over the farm, including solar water heating, a biomass boiler and solar electricity – so it's little wonder that the site was awarded a Sustainable Tourism Gold Award for Carmarthenshire in 2015/16.

Eco accolades aside, there's plenty to tempt you to this spellbinding place. Undulating, verdant hills, gently flowing brooks, enchanting wooded glens – Ceridwen has views, and then some. After that there's the accommodation. Besides several converted farm buildings (including a refurbished calving shed and an über-luxurious central house), glamping guests have a choice of four hand-crafted Welsh yurts, a gypsy caravan, the Caban Bach wooden pod or the Hop Shack cabin. Each of the yurts sleep up to four, so

they're ideal for a small family. Sitting in sweet seclusion in a wildflower-strewn apple orchard, these fully furnished abodes are the very essence of 'getting away from it all'. For those with more amorous intentions, the gypsy Cwtch (Welsh for a heartfelt cuddle) is a lovingly restored 19th-century Romany wagon with views to die for. The Cwtch features all the antiquated charms of the traveller heritage – Welsh woollen blankets, china collectables, a brass mantelpiece over the warming range stove. There have been more than a couple of proposals made from this enviable spot – so don't be surprised if you find yourself returning a year hence for your own nuptials.

Whether here as part of a group or seeking the solace and seclusion of a countryside break, Ceridwen radiates a wholly inclusive, laid-back attitude. You may choose to indulge in a few of the many varied workshops on offer, from yoga to creative writing. If the latter, you'll not be short of inspiration for some suitably purple prose. As you admire the idyll before you, red kites circling overhead, you might like to consider that Ceridwen was the enchantress of Welsh medieval legend said to possess the cauldron of Poetic Inspiration. How apt a name for a setting to whose charms you will soon succumb.

The Ceridwen Centre, Drefelin, Drefach-Felindre, Llandysul, Carmarthenshire SA44 5XE 01559 370517 ceridwencentre.co.uk

❀ Four yurts (each sleeping a family of 4), a gypsy Cwtch wagon (for couples), Caban Bach (wooden eco-pod sleeping 2), The Hop Shack (wood-clad cabin sleeping 4–5), plus regular camping pitches. Yurts are furnished with rugs, cushions and blankets, copper-topped tables, wood-burning stoves and beds. Shared cooking facilities in the summer house, with a 2-ring gas stove, all cooking equipment, a sink and fridge. There's a choice of toilet facilities – a compost loo close by the yurts, 2 conventional loos and showers down in the farmyard and a new eco-loo shepherd's hut with 2 female loos and a shower, 1 male loo and a shower and a urinal. There's also an onsite bike park with bikes for hire.

❀ Soak up this stunning corner of West Wales via the Gwili Steam Railway (01267 238213). Brechfa Forest, a 30-minute drive away, has cracking mountain biking trails, circular walks and 2 great salmon and trout fishing spots in the Tywi and Cothi rivers.

❀ Simone is happy to whip up cakes and desserts for special occasions and also hosts regular summer pizza nights. The site is licensed to sell alcohol, and varied stock and organic veg boxes from the farm are available in season. The John y Gwas (01559 370469) is a quirky little local just a mile down the hill and is well worth the slog back up, especially for ale afficionados.

❀ Open all year; yurts late-March–Oct.

❀ Yurts from £155 for 2 nights; Cwtch from £185 for 2 nights; Caban Bach from £147 for 2 nights. Hop Shack from £198 for 2 nights.

cwtch camp

Everybody knows about the beauty of the Pembrokeshire Coast – Wales' most filmic stretch of seaboard plays host to some 7.2 million tourists every year. But while most visitors to this breathtaking national park congregate around St Davids and Fishguard, the Daugleddau Estuary is one of Pembrokeshire's more overlooked coastal gems. Often dubbed 'The Secret Waterway', its secluded waters are actually made up of four different rivers, collectively combining between steep wooded banks, topped by Norman castles and teeming with widlife. It is along one of the River Cleddau's snaking tributaries, by the Westfield Pill Nature Reserve, that another of southern Pembrokeshire's hidden treasures is found.

Cwtch Camp couldn't be more aptly named. With its title taken from the Welsh for 'snug' or 'heartfelt cuddle', this cosy little spot is secreted within three acres of bucolic spruce woodland. Comprising three hand-crafted wooden eco-cabins (the titular cwtches), this low-impact campsite marries the classic wild camping experience with the luxury of a fully insulated cabin. The facilities are surprisingly ample (communal kitchen, hot shower, flushing toilet) but it is off-grid, so don't forget that torch!

Each Cwtch is handmade, using locally milled, sustainably sourced timber. They're bright, secure and roomy yet cosy. There are even sound-insulated roof tiles so, should it rain, you'll be soothed with a gentle pitter-patter instead of a roaring Biblical downpour. Though Welsh in name, these cannily-crafted cabans are a model of Scandinavian ergonomics, handily sleeping a couple or family of four. All have a south-facing deck, allowing you to bask in the over 1700 hours of sunshine Pembrokeshire enjoys every year.

After you've spent a day foraging in this abundant countryside, or losing hours on the beaches of St Brides Bay, Cwtch's cosy abodes are perfect for snuggling up under thick Welsh wool blankets, with that special someone. Because everybody needs a hug sometimes...

Cwtch Camp, Barn Lane, Rosemarket, Pembrokeshire SA73 1LH 07525 779454 cwtchcamping.co.uk

❄ Three timber eco-pods; Caban Cariad and Caban Bach each sleeping 2 in a double bed. Ty Cwtch sleeps 3 adults/2 adults and 2 children in bunks. An additional bell tent sleeps 3 adults/2 adults and 2 children. Facilities include a toilet, hot water shower and a fully-equipped communal kitchen with a double gas hob (utensils, etc provided). Cool-box topped up with ice provided in each cabin. Exclusive site hire available (maximum 14 guests). No electricity. Lighting provided by solar candles, campfires and lanterns.

❄ The Pembrokeshire Coast Path is the big attraction here but there are plenty of lesser-known trails, including the Landsker Borderlands Trail, which circles the eastern bank of the Daugleddau Estuary. Bosherton Lilly Ponds (01646 661359), Picton Castle & Gardens (01437 751326) and Carew Castle & Tidal Mill (01646 651782) are all well worth a visit. The Brunel Cycle Trail is a gentle 9-mile cycle path between Haverfordwest and Neyland. Pembrokeshire's beaches are legendary: Barafundle Bay, Little Haven and Druidstone all have their own unique character, and Newgale Beach is great for watersports.

❄ Guests are greeted with a welcome hamper on arrival comprising fresh farm eggs, a freshly-baked loaf, tea, coffee and milk ready for breakfast. Onsite catering can also be arranged for groups hiring the entire site. The Bar at Neyland Marina (01646 602550) is just a 30-minute walk (or 10-minute cycle). Its seafood-centric menu uses locally caught fish and the views overlooking Westfield Pill set off the atmosphere perfectly.

❄ Open March–Nov.

❄ Eco-cabins £95 per night; bell tents start from £75 per night.

the yurt farm

Yurts. Just a few short years ago they were a rare breed in the Welsh countryside, an exotic novelty. Now, suddenly, they're everywhere. But not all yurts are created equal, and thankfully those at the Yurt Farm are a cut above many of the rest, a collection of just five yurts put together by thoughtful owners Thea and Laurie in a careful, planned-out way, then nurtured and loved into existence. Breathing new life into a forgotten corner of a large organic farm in Ceredigion, the Yurt Farm is, however, less about the accommodation and more about the fully immersive experience of this off-beat, off-grid, off-the-beaten-track hideaway.

A spacious hay meadow gives each yurt as much room as some other campsites might give 30 tents. The yurts are warm and cosy, not to mention impeccably well maintained, as is the beautifully converted railway carriage that sits on a separate natural bench with lovely views of the Cambrian Mountains. The location of this glampsite is perfect – ridiculously remote and enveloped in the sort of rich, green countryside for which Wales is famous. And the love is evident everywhere; a welcome basket of tasty veg for guests; unique four-poster beds fashioned out of trees; and wheelbarrows on hand for transporting your gear (vehicles are not allowed on site).

There's a cosy communal wood cabin with cooking facilities, tables, chairs and board games for rainy days. However, most of your glamping time will no doubt be spent outdoors. In all, there are 150 acres to be discovered, criss-crossed by a network of farm trails, and children are free to explore, make dens, hide in the long grass, play in the sand, hang off rope swings, collect eggs, be licked by cows and gorge themselves silly on the blackcurrants and gooseberries that grow in the yurt meadow.

With the striking Cambrian mountains as a backdrop to this enchanting place, there's no doubt this beautiful, remote location enhances the blissed-out go-slow vibe. Even if it's those quirky little yurts that brings you here in the first place, it'll be the welcome, the hospitality and the low-impact philosophy that'll keep you coming back.

The Yurt Farm, Crynfryn, Penuwch, Tregaron, Ceredigion SY25 6RE 01974 821594 theyurtfarm.co.uk

❊ The yurts sleep between 1 and 6 people; the railway carriage sleeps 4. All are exceptionally well equipped, with futons, bedding and cooking equipment including gas hob, a basket of farm goodies, tea and coffee-making facilities and a first-aid kit, a wood-burning stove plus logs and kindling. Outside each yurt there's a BBQ or firepit and a picnic table. The cabin has a 4-ring gas hob, more cooking equipment, board games and lots of extra bits and bobs, such as toasted sandwich-makers to use on the fire. Next door is the compost loo and solar shower. There's also a sandpit, swing, a woodshed yurt for extra firewood and an honesty farm shop with meat, veg and jam for sale.
❊ One of the highlights of the area is watching the famous dolphins of Cardigan Bay. You can get a boat from nearby Newquay. Details of a whole raft of days out can be found in the cabin, including Oakwood Theme Park (01834 891376), around an hour's drive away, and Dolaucothi Gold Mines (01558 825146), where you can try your hand at panning for gold.
❊ Just over 3 miles away, the traditional Rhos Yr Hafod Inn (01974 272644) at Cross Inn has the tiny windows, thick walls, crackling fires and oak beams that all old pubs should have. Foodies will want to head a bit further to Aberaeron Harbour and the delightful Harbourmaster Hotel (01545 570755). For an open fire, great ale and food go to Y Talbot (01974 298208) in Tregaron.
❊ Open April–Sept.
❊ Weekly rates in both yurts and train carriage from £420–£690; 3-night breaks from £220.

eco retreats

Run by reiki healers ChaNan and husband Michael, Eco Retreats is an upmarket campsite aimed at those campers who need to take a break from the stresses and strains of modern living. Three fully equipped tipis, one 18-ft yurt and one 20-ft yurt set up especially for families are hidden away in a stunning, remote forest – as a place to chill, you won't find many options that are more horizontal than this.

The site's theme is peace and tranquillity, with a healthy dose of eco-living thrown in. To get you into the mood, the camping experience even includes optional sessions of reiki healing in the comfort of your own tipi or yurt and a soothing meditation as the sun sets. The dwellings are furnished in a relaxed, luxurious and romantic way – from sheepskins strewn across the double bed to tea lights scattered on every surface. A pack of organic edible treats greets you on arrival and all the necessary cooking paraphernalia is conveniently to hand. Heating is from both a wood-burning chimenea or stove inside and an open fire outside.

Each of the dwellings is set in its own idyllic location, where your only neighbour is the great outdoors. Beneath the stars or a leafy canopy of mature trees, each abode is accompanied by a wood-fired outdoor bathtub where you can bathe to a soundtrack of birdsong or spend evenings deciphering the various constellations.

The Meadow Yurt is the best family-sized option, with two single futons as well as the double bed. The surrounding meadow also makes a great play space for children, carpeted as it is with wildflowers in spring. The Waterfall Tipi, on the other hand, is a fairly steep 10-minute walk across the river then up through a wood, carpeted with bluebells in spring, with the waterfall itself just down the slope behind. The Forest Tipi has the most private location. It's a longer, slightly more strenuous walk up a steep hill, but enjoys a breathtaking spot in a clearing in the forest. The River Yurt, which is slightly more spacious than the tipis, is nestled down close to the river – an ideal spot for paddling, or even a full dip if you're up for it.

The newest tipi is the only one with a Welsh name – Cwm Onnen, meaning Ash Valley (as in the tree) – and stands at the top of the site commanding an impressive view of the whole valley and hills beyond. It's easily accessible – you can drive up the farm track and leave the car just a short walk away across the field.

Envelop yourself in the Eco Retreats experience. Leave all your usual gizmos at home – don't take your mobile, laptop, radio, iPod or even your guitar. Just doze off listening to the fire crackling – and wake up to birdsong, running water and the wind in the trees. It's Zen and the art of camping.

Eco Retreats, Plas Einion, Furnace, Machynlleth, Powys SY20 8PG (office address only) 01654 781375 ecoretreats.co.uk

❀ Each tipi and yurt is kitted out with everything you need, except food. A private eco-loo and mountain spring shower are on the doorstep.
❀ You won't want to leave. But there's always the Centre for Alternative Technology (01654 705950); the Corris Craft Centre (01654 761584) a couple of miles up the A487; the Museum of Modern Art at Machynlleth (01654 703355); or tea shops by the beach in nearby Aberdyfi.
❀ The Slaters Arms in Corris (01654 761324) is a brilliant local pub just a few miles from Cader Idris, serving hearty food as well as a good selection of real ales. The Wynnstay Hotel at Machynlleth (01654 702941) is a gastropub with a great atmosphere and good food in the bar, plus a separate pizza restaurant. The Number 21 bistro (01654 703382), on the High Street in Machynlleth, is another local highlight.
❀ Open late March–late Oct.
❀ A basic weekend break for 2 starts at £279. The full package, which includes Reiki, meditation and a small organic hamper, is an extra £110. Extra nights are £70. Children aged 15 and under are free but there is a small supplement for older children and extra adults.

graig wen

Situated in the south-west corner of the Snowdonia National Park, there's no doubt that Graig Wen enjoys one of the best glamping locations in the whole of Wales, set among 45 acres of its own wild woods and meadows, and with amazing views over the Mawddach Estuary curling down to Cardigan Bay far below. Only a few years ago the land here was filled with old caravans, car batteries and monster conifers, but new owners Sarah and John have transformed the place, hand-building two yurts from ash trees found on their own land and kitting them out with quirky furniture and textiles. They've also added regular camping pitches, more glamping options and even a holiday cottage. It's a great place to stay, no question.

So impressive was the site's transformation that they won the Green Snowdonia Award in 2009 for 'Most Sustainable Campsite', and rightly so. Well-maintained facilities with hot showers are kept spick and span. Viewing benches overlooking Mawddach Estuary offer the best seat in the house at sunset o'clock – especially given Snowdonia's 'Dark Skies' status – and a simple camp shop stocks local ales and other essentials; you can also book breakfast hampers and chilled bubbly for arrival. The pitches themselves are positioned to suit most tastes, with space for tourers and tents along with four glamping options. Isolated and sheltered among dense woodland, there are two yurts and a 'caban' timber structure which has a rather Scandinavian feel – its glazed walls provide magnificent views but can be shuttered for when things get a little more intimate. There's also a furnished bell tent for hire during the summer.

A geocache trail provides a way of exploring the site's woods and streams, and learning a bit about the area's slate-mining heritage, while more intrepid explorers can tackle Cader Idris – the spectacular mountain at the back of Graig Wen, where the crowds tend to be much smaller than you get on the summit of Snowdon. According to legend, if you spend the night on the top of Cader, you'll come down a poet or, yes, a madman.

You can cycle all the way to Fairbourne beach in Barmouth without even seeing a road, and virtually the entire route to Dolgellau in the other direction is road-free, too. In addition to the cycle track, there's another family cycling path, plus more challenging mountain-bike trails at nearby Coed-y-Brenin.

Back at camp, after a hard day's cycling, it's time to light a campfire. After burning rubber all day, burning a few marshmallows on sticks seems like a well-earned treat.

Graig Wen, Arthog, Nr Dolgellau, Gwynedd LL39 1YP
01341 250482 graigwen.co.uk

❋ Two yurts (respectively sleeping 2 and 5), a cabin (sleeping 2) and a bell tent in July/Aug along with regular camping pitches. Unusually, the yurts are dog-friendly. There are a couple of rope swings, plenty of trees to climb and occasional wildlife walks. There are 2 unisex showers. Campfires allowed (bag of logs £5). You can hire bikes on site (£20) or at Dolgellau Cycles (01341 423332).

❋ Clambering up Cader Idris (892m) is a great option, and the family-friendly Pony Path makes it manageable for all – the campsite even gives a certificate to children under 10 who make it to the summit. Alternatively, walk straight off the site along the stunning (and flat) waterside Mawddach Trail to reach the seaside treats of Barmouth. You can also cycle along the estuary to Fairbourne beach, and there are more challenging mountain-bike rides at nearby Coed-y-Brenin (01341 440747), around 5 miles north of Dolgellau. There are lots of wild swimming spots too – ask about the Blue Lake, a local favourite – and the zip wires and trampolines of Llechwedd Slate Quarry (01766 830306) are just half an hour away.

❋ The owners sell eggs, ice cream, marshmallows and breakfast hampers in high season. Stock up on local produce and tasty treats at the Country Market on Thursday mornings, or the Farmers' Market on the third Sunday of every month, both in Dolgellau. There's good pub grub at The George III Hotel (01341 422525) 5 minutes' drive away or an hour's delightful walk away along the estuary cycle trail. Locally produced lamb, beef and fish can be enjoyed outside in view of the estuary.

❋ Open Easter–end Oct.

❋ Yurts and cabins from £160 for a 2-night break. Bell tent from £65 per night.

bryn dinas camping pods

Anyone born west of Offa's Dyke knows the tale of Beddgelert. The story goes that Welsh prince Llywelyn the Great once had his palace here. Upon returning from a hunting trip without his faithful hound, Gelert, the prince was greeted by the blood-stained dog. Anxious Llywelyn went to find his young infant son but, finding the boy's crib empty and smeared with blood, ferociously plunged his sword into the dog's side, believing him to have savaged the royal heir. Gelert's dying yelp was met with the child's cry, whereupon the prince found the body of a mighty wolf which Gelert had slain. After realising his mistake, it is said that the prince never smiled again and the town's name is a byword for any grave error of judgement. Ironic, then, that, unlike poor luckless Llywelyn, a stay at this Beddgelert glampsite could be just about the wisest decision you'll ever make.

Follow the Glaslyn river upstream from Beddgelert and you'll soon reach a charming 18th-century farmhouse set between the tranquil twin lakes at Dinas and Gwynant.

This is the home of Red Dragon Holidays and, more specifically, the Bryn Dinas Camping Pods – five custom-built pods that sleep two-a-piece and are equipped with all the basics you could require for a tentless trekking holiday. Think of this as a well-maintained base camp for tackling the mighty peaks of the Snowdonia National Park. Facilities are functional rather than luxurious but more than adequate, with two self-contained bathrooms 10 metres from the pods, a communal kitchenette and common area (with Wi-Fi and internet access) and a life-saving laundry/drying room. Besides, this is Wales' outdoors capital, and you didn't come here to be pampered now did you?

Wholehearted hostess Claire is happy to prepare you a packed lunch or organise bike hire. She knows all the best walking routes and, more importantly, the best local pubs. In homage to poor old Gelert, Claire also welcomes dogs to the site and in the camping pods. And then there's Beddgelert itself. This much-garlanded town is one of Wales' best located, with unspoiled Anglesey, the golden sands of Cardigan Bay and, of course, epic Snowdonia all within easy reach. Bryn Dinas Camping Pods is without question the perfect base for exploring this truly amazing pocket of Wales.

Bryn Dinas Camping Pods, Bryn Dinas, Nantgwynant, Nr Beddgelert, Caernarfon, Gwynedd LL55 4NH 01766 890351
bryndinascampingpods.co.uk

❁ Five pods, each sleeping 2, and including twin beds and 4 electric points. There is also 'the Dragon's Lair' a larger 4-person bunkroom beside the main communal building. There are 2 self-contained heated bathrooms within 10m of the pods, each with toilet, sink and shower, onsite laundry with coin-operated washing machine and tumble dryer; drying room, community room with a PC with free internet access. Wi-Fi available in pod (chargeable). BBQ area, small kitchenette with fridge/ freezer, combination microwave and toaster.

❁ The Watkin Path, leading right to the top of Snowdon, is just 300m from the site. You can also hire mountain bikes from Beddgelert Bikes (01766 890434). The Ffestiniog Welsh Highland Railways (01766 516000) are a wonderfully nostalgic way to take in the stunning Snowdonia scenery. You can hop on at Beddgelert and go around the foot of mighty Snowdon, through the beautiful Aberglaslyn Pass and on to Porthmadog. Nearby, Zipworld Snowdonia (01248 601444) is the northern hemipshere's longest zipwire, suspended 1800ft above the disused Penrhyn slate quarry.

❁ The excellent Caffi Gwynant (01766 890855) is 300m up the road and serves a range of hearty Welsh breakfasts, substantial sandwiches, and other inventive meals – the perfect sustenance for hitting the slopes. Beddgelert Bistro Antiques (01766 890543) does delicious homemade cakes. The village also boasts a couple of decent, welcoming pubs, including the Tanronnen Inn (01766 890347) and the Saracen's Head (01766 890329), both of which serve food.

❁ Open all year.

❁ Pods from £38 per night, Dragon's Lair from £65 per night.

anglesey tipi and yurt holidays

Mam Cymru. The Mother of Wales. Whatever you call it, Anglesey – separated from the mainland only by the narrow Menai Strait – epitomises the rich heritage of Wales. It has seen Celtic, Viking and medieval settlers, and remains a predominantly Welsh-speaking island. You can almost feel the earth pulsate in time to 'Hen Wlad Fy Nhadau'.

Anglesey has yet to be overrun by luxury camping options, but if you head to the east of the island, just outside Brynteg, you'll find the hidden oasis of Anglesey Tipi and Yurts has the glamping side of things very well covered.

Refreshingly, owners Charlie and Ela know that creating a great campsite takes more than just plonking a few yurts and tipis in a field, and this place is clearly a labour of love. Not that they'd get complacent, of course. It's clear to see that this is a constantly evolving, living, breathing site, and they work year-round to ensure that it keeps on improving.

Charlie and Ela are attentive hosts. There are wheelbarrows on hand to transport your weekend bags to your accommodation and a hefty bag of firewood for the start of your stay. Ela's recently honed weaving skills have been put to good use in creating a winding tunnel for kids to run through, and there's a patch of woodland left just wild enough for you to feel like you're the first person to discover it. There are two tipis and three yurts dotted around the main camping space. Inside each, you'll find plenty of cooking implements, plus enough fluffy cushions and sheepskin rugs to make your dwelling delightfully welcoming. Each yurt has a wood-burning stove, each tipi a chiminea, and all have small BBQs outside, plus there's a communal firepit and a sheltered area where campers gather at dusk. They get extra Brownie points for their eco credentials, too. Recycling? Check. Compost loo? Check.

Anglesey Tipi and Yurt Holidays is the camping equivalent to chicken noodle soup – a great pick-me-up, and you feel a whole lot better after trying it. This is sustainable camping for peace-seeking visitors, and the best way to discover what makes it so magical is to come and soak up the ambience yourself. Once you've snuggled into a woodland hammock, leaving the site will be the last thing on your mind, but for some truly breathtaking views, the Isle of Anglesey Coastal Path is worth tearing yourself away for, with scores of sweeping beaches and towering cliffs on hand to discover.

Anglesey Tipi & Yurt Holidays, Cae'r Gaseg, Brynteg, Anglesey LL78 8JT 01248 853162 angleseytipis.co.uk

❀ Two tipis and 3 yurts, the former with chimineas inside, the latter with wood-burning stoves (first bundle of wood is free). Accommodation contains small gas stoves, cutlery and cooking utensils, a BBQ and a mix of double beds and futon-style beds. There are 2 flush toilets in the cabin facility block and 2 compost loos in the woods. The cabin also has 2 hot showers, a nappy-changing table, electricity points and sinks, with plenty of room for kids to sit and play. There's also a wild wood with footpaths and hammocks. Campfires allowed in a designated area.

❀ The site might feel a fair way out of town (though the nearest shops are still within easy driving distance), but that just adds to the charm. Follow the Isle of Anglesey Coastal Path to explore the stunning coastline, or hop on to a Puffin Island cruise (01248 810251) for a different perspective. Budding lepidopterists will enjoy the butterflies at Pili Palas (01248 712474), while thrill-seekers can scale new heights at the Beacon Climbing Centre (08454 508222), near Llanberis. Visit the Oriel Kyffin Williams art gallery at Llangefni (01248 724444) or the village of Beaumaris with its UNESCO medieval castle and Victorian pier. There's also the mock-Italian village of Portmeirion, famously used as the set for 1960s TV series, *The Prisoner*, which is a 45-minute drive.

❀ The Menai Bridge is a fantastic hub for foodies. There are heaps of great local producers around, plus a monthly farmers' market. Relax in Grade-II listed style at the Bull Hotel (01248 722119), which serves well-priced hearty mains, or frequent the superb Bay Cafe at Beach Road, Benllech (01248 852700), for great sea views and excellent home-cooked food, including great puddings.

❀ April–end Sept.

❀ Two-person tipi £55–£60 per night, 4-person tipi £70–£80. Four-person yurt £80–£90 a night; the Mongolian yurts (sleeping up to 5) £90–£110 per night. Two-night minimum stay.

mill house farm

Mill House Farm, Cruckmeole, Hanwood, Shrewsbury, Shropshire SY5 8JN 01743 860576 millhousefarm.org

---

❋ A beautiful washroom unit has a compost toilet, outdoor shower, sink and washing area. All bed linen and towels provided (if you bring an extra tent you'll need to bring the bedding, or it can be provided at £7 per set). There's a powered cool-box, a 2-ring gas stove and outside a firepit, Dutch oven and BBQ with a welcome pack of fuel. A trampoline, rope swing, swing bench by the brook and a fun-sized football pitch provide entertainment. The Rae Brook river runs along one side of the farm and they own the fishing rights – though you'll need to bring your own gear.

❋ Easy access to public footpaths. Head south towards the hills or an hour and 10 minutes walking north leads you to Shrewsbury, a lovely medieval town full of independent shops and restaurants. A 10-minute drive south, the Shropshire Hills AONB (01588 674080) also has fantastic walking routes, including the Stiperstones, where you can gently climb through the heather to 'the devil's chair' and are rewarded with fabulous views. There is a clearly marked car park for the Stiperstones Nature Reserve. Continue further up the road to an excellent pub, the Stiperstones Inn (01743 791327).

❋ Guests arrive to a welcome basket of necessities to keep them going until they get to the shops (eggs, milk, bread, butter, tea, coffee and oil). Pub-wise, the nearest is The Cock Inn (01743 860392) just 20-minutes' walk away. It's rather basic, so for the best food and atmosphere, The Nag's Head (01743 790060), on the main road to Pontesbury, is recommended.

❋ Open April–end Oct.

❋ From £75 per night in low season, £85 in high season.

It's like a last round zinger in the local pub quiz… 'How many glamping wagons can lay claim to hosting Julius Caesar, King John, Henry VIII and Richard III?' Heads turn, eyebrows lower, snorts of frustration pervade the room. Clearly it's a very stupid question. Yet parked up in a beautiful wild grass meadow in Shropshire, the Oddsocks glamping cart at Mill House Farm has done just that – albeit in the trick-answer sort of way you would expect from a pub quiz. Thanks to its former life as a travelling stage for Shakespeare productions – an exact replica of those used from the 10th–16th centuries

– it has seen them all and then some, with even the likes of Romeo and Juliet appearing on board over the years. But after a quarter of a century in motion and over 150,000 miles under its belt, the stage, now roofed, contained and adorably decorated inside, has retired to the pastures of rural England.

Set in a large, oval-shaped field, skirted on its northern edge by gently flowing Rae Brook, the Oddsocks Cart is a strikingly cosy-looking cabin with a shape reminiscent of traditional shepherd's huts. From the front, though, a rectangular decking area creates a more unique form and the warm-looking, auburn wood panels give it an almost summerhouse feel. However you choose to describe it, the indisputable fact is that it's an enviable place to stay.

Inside, the light, white walls increase the sense of space, while a folding table and a sofa bed allow you extra room. There is a sink, two hobs and a welcome hamper of important goodies like tea, coffee, oil and other essentials, while outside a round Weber BBQ is ideal for late summer evenings. Inside, of course, that essential bit of kit – a wood-burning stove – is also present. So if the weather takes a turn for the worse, you're well kitted out for cosy evenings with hot chocolate and a good novel.

Most of the time, however, is spent outdoors. The rope swing that dangles invitingly from a central tree draws children like a magnet, while footpaths lead out directly from the farm into the rolling countryside beyond – and eventually to Shrewsbury, the county town and an excellent spot to explore. From farm to centre takes around an hour and 20 minutes.

The best way to get the inside scoop is to talk to Adrian and Gemma, the affable owners of Mill House Farm who first met each other on tour with the Oddsocks Theatre Company. As you'd expect from two thespians, they're a wonderfully friendly pair, with lots of local knowledge – of walking routes, pubs and other handy bits of info – while scholarly discussions of Shakespeare are equally welcome. And who knows what gems of information might help you out in the next pub quiz?

the dandelion hideaway

As you head down Lount Road, surrounded by a patchwork of fields and infrequent tractors, it feels like you're pioneering on a journey deep into forgotten Leicestershire. Time itself seems to stand still, until you discover the Dandelion Hideaway, an idyllic glamping Eden run by John and Sharon Earp, two of the most welcoming owners you're ever likely to meet. The hard-working duo have done their hosting homework to create something truly special here; indeed the combination of fairytale romance, five-star indulgence and outdoor adventure makes the Dandelion Hideaway one of the UK's finest glamping getaways. Set on a working farm teeming with livestock (goats, hens, Shetland ponies), the site's six canvas cottages are thoughtfully located in the heart of the farm, all with far-reaching countryside views. The interiors have a wonderfully earthy feel, enhancing the site's natural concept. There's a traditional farmhouse kitchen and wood-burning stove inside each one, along with country furniture, faded linens, a whistling kettle and other lovely little touches that add to the rustic atmosphere. In keeping with the splendid setting, each cottage comes armed with a luxurious free-standing roll-top bath), flushing loo and separate sink – perfect for those not fancying the morning trudge to the shower block.

Dandelion Hideaway is perfectly located for the nearby National Forest, an ambitious project to generate new spaces of sustainable woodland across Staffordshire, Derbyshire and Leicestershire, while back at the site guests are invited to get involved in the woodland survival courses run throughout the summer, along with educational farm tours with John, while kids can help milk the goats, collect eggs and groom the friendly Shetland ponies. One animal less likely to make an appearance is the badger, but the site has its very own watching hide. Take the unique opportunity to get up close to these night-loving creatures before heading back to your oh-so-cosy canvas cottage.

The Dandelion Hideaway, Osbaston House Farm, Lount Road, Osbaston, Leicestershire CV13 0HR 01455 292888 thedandelionhideaway.co.uk

❀ Five luxury canvas cottages (sleeping 6), complete with farmhouse furniture, living area, bathroom with a roll-top bath and shower, kitchen dresser, butler's sink with brass taps, chunky wooden worktops, fridge and wood-burning fire (with oven and stove). Also a private and romantic cottage (Bluebells) with a roomy bedroom, sitting/dining room, nostalgic toys and dreamy books, French day bed, antique gramophone and large veranda, accompanied by, Bluebell's Nest, the adjacent, elevated tree house that sleeps 2, with antique iron beds, loo and sink – and a private, eco-friendly wooden hot tub!
❀ The site is perfectly located for the National Forest, where more than eight million saplings have taken root, and all sorts of visitor attractions are also sprouting up, including Conkers, an award-winning nature centre. However, the forest's real draw is its abundance of walks and bike trails. Summer afternoons can be spent exploring the endless acres (193,000 to be precise) of colourful heathlands, imposing woodlands and bubbling streams. Other nearby tourist attractions include Bosworth Battlefield and its educational heritage centre (01455 290429). Kids can test their archery skills and dress in traditional medieval armour.
❀ The converted Old Cow Shed is open exclusively for guests, offering a wide range of meals, drinks and snacks on an old-fashioned honesty account basis. The Gate Inn (01455 290502) is only a 15-minute walk away and boasts a range of classic pub dishes.
❀ Open March–Nov.
❀ Cottages £725–£1150 a week, £575–£750 a weekend (Fri–Mon), £500–£700 midweek (Mon–Fri).

mulino pods

In the centre of a curved oak picture frame stands a tree, just going out of bloom and now rich with the greens of summer. Beneath it, the ground slopes away, falling into a valley that rises once more on the other side, rolling away into a backdrop that's crowned by a long, dark lake. Though the lake is several miles away, the sun on its surface makes it stand out among the hills, a focal point in this bucolic rural scene. The oak frame around this picture, though, is not hanging on a wall, but *is* the

wall: the curved wooden exterior of a comfortable Mulino pod. Pull the latch, open the glass door and feel the Derbyshire breeze…

Set up in 2009, Mulino Lodge Farm plays a huge role in shaping the landscape around you, from the Suffolk Mule and Charollais Sheep in the fields to the dry stone walls that stripe the hills in the distance. To the north, further into the Peak District, the farm is having an impact too, grazing highland cattle in conservation projects. In the heart of this enviable countryside location lie two glamping pods that are more than just a farmer's afterthought, with all the facilities you could want for a stay in the hills. Along with local information, maps, games and the like, there is a well-equipped outdoor kitchen area, private bathrooms and washing facilities for muddy boots, bikes or dogs. Touches like the spices and essentials in the kitchen store cupboard or complimentary tea and coffee make the difference, especially if you arrive late, disorganised and a little out of sorts.

As with most rural spots in England there's a real community vibe around these parts and never more so than when you're waking up on the local farm. It's a mile-and-a-half walk to the village pub, a pleasant cross-country stroll to the Red Lion, and the market town of Ashbourne, home to a host of independent shops and a starting-point for lots of local trails, is well worth a visit too if you don't mind the 10-minute drive. Meanwhile, back at base, those hanging up their walking boots for the day should chat to Craig, who knows the land well and is more than happy to give you a tour of the farm. When you're back around the BBQ, enjoying that view, you'll be able to appreciate it all the more.

Mulino Lodge, Kniveton, Ashbourne, Derbyshire DE6 1JR 01335 216220 mulinopods.co.uk

❋ Two pods (sleeping up to 3 adults or 2 adults, 2 children) and a third, larger pod (sleeping up to 6). All include a double bed (with space for the children or third adult on an additional bed), small fridge, toaster and kettle, eco-power points, lighting and a heater in cooler months. Outside there's seating, a table, use of a firepit and BBQ area and a drinking water tap, plus a covered communal kitchen fully equipped with everything you need plus some essential ingredients in the cupboard store. Each individual bathroom has a power shower, WC, basin, mirror and heater. A dressing area has hairdryer facilities and a shaving point. A small, central room provides local information, maps and leaflets, free Wi-Fi, a book swap, games and a toy box for the kids. Plus there's an honesty shop with charcoal, fire-lighters and other basics. The site also has an outdoor wash area for bikes, dogs and boots.

❋ Carsington Water (01629 540478) is the most dominant point in the landscape, where you can try sailing, windsurfing and other water sports. For something less energetic, visit the historic market town of Ashbourne, 17th-century Sudbury Hall (01283 585337) or the charming gardens of Ilam Park (01335 350503).

❋ There are farmers markets' at Leek (3rd Weds and Sat of the month), Bakewell (last Sat of the month), Wirksworth (1st Sat of the month) and Buxton (1st Thurs of the month). It's a long but pleasant walk (1.5 miles) to the village pub, the Red Lion (01334 345554) which serves great food in a warm, friendly atmosphere.

❋ Open all year.

❋ Weekends (Fri–Mon) £230; midweek (Mon–Fri) £240; weekly (Fri–Fri or Mon–Mon) £410. Dogs (max 2, Damson and Lavender pods), £25 per stay.

secret cloud house holidays

Secret Cloud's yurts are just the spot for a guilt-free, luxury glamping splurge. The four yurts, Elderflower, Foxglove, Rosehip and Blackberry and the new year-round Bilberry Lodge (an Arctic-inspired wooden cabin) sit in a flat field, shared only by a few Hebridean sheep and surrounded by farmland, with panoramic views across the Manifold Valley and heathlands of Ipstones Edge. Catherine and her partner Ian run the site and have lovingly furnished each yurt with wooden floors, a handmade double bed, a table and chairs for candlelit dining and a wood-burning stove with a supply of logs. They are snugly fitted out with feather down duvets, Egyptian cotton sheets, fluffy towels, Secret Cloud bathrobes, Staffordshire wool blankets and sheepskin rugs. Glamping guests are also treated to a locally sourced breakfast hamper, and each yurt has its own private wood-fired hot tub. Guests are also welcome to use the wood-fuelled barrel sauna, and the site now offers massage treatments by candlelight in 'Shepherds Rest' in front of the roaring fire. Despite the luxury, this is also an eco-friendly site, endorsed by the Peak District National Park each year since 2011. Each yurt has its own compost loo, the shower rooms are fitted with solar panels and insulated with sheep's wool, while lighting is candlelight and solar fairy lights. Every effort is also made to source products locally, from the yurts themselves to the handmade toiletries and the sustainable Staffordshire charcoal for the BBQ.

Secret Cloud House Holidays, Limestone View Farm, Stoney Lane, Cauldon, Staffordshire ST10 3EP
07845 939603 secretcloudhouseholidays.co.uk

❀ Four luxury yurts sleeping up to 4 people with a handmade double bed (and a pull-out bed and air mattress for families). Bilberry Lodge sleeps 2 (or provides a communal area if a group books out the whole site). The washrooms have 2 large shower rooms with hot showers and hand-washing basins, and there is a washing-up sink and drainer. Each yurt has a gas stove, wood-burning stove and cool-box; and there is a private compost loo in a wooden hut as well as outdoor seating and a BBQ. Campfires are allowed.

❀ The site is just beneath Ipstones Edge, where the Staffordshire Wildlife Trust manages the nature reserve with the help of a small herd of Shetland ponies. The Trentham Estate (01782 646646) is around half an hour away by car and has gardens, the Monkey Forest and 'aerial extreme' high ropes; Alton Towers (0871 222 3330) is also just 5 minutes away.

❀ Catherine recommends the Yew Tree (01538 308348) in Cauldon, which serves good ales and is also something of an antiques museum; it even has a couple of pairs of Queen Victoria's stockings! There's also the Marquis of Granby (01538 266462) in Ipstones, a couple of miles away, which does excellent food.

❀ Yurts open March–Oct, Bilberry Lodge all year.

❀ April–Oct £345 for a 3-night weekend stay; midweek stays from £250 for 2 nights.

stanley villa farm camping

'A tranquil lakeside glampsite just 15 minutes from Blackpool?' you probe incredulously. No, dear camper, we're not a few tent pegs short of a full set. Bounded by the Bowland Hills to the east, the Irish Sea to the west, Morecambe Bay to the north and the Ribble Estuary to the south, the Lancashire Fylde is a nutrient-rich alluvial peninsula where flora and fauna abound. And it is here that the industrious folk from Stanley Villa Farm have been creating their new 'Camping Bugs' site.

The colourful purpose built 'bugs' are fully insulated and equipped (though you'll need to bring your own bedding) and offer perfect, den-like digs for tired little ones after they've been exploring the sprawling fields. The communal Lakeside Lodge has everything you need for a hassle-free stay, including washing and cooking facilities and a large common room.

The centrepiece of the site is the five-acre lake. The Flyde Trout Fishery welcomes all levels of anglers to fish the various breeds of trout. It's not unusual to see wild deer as well as the usual suspects (rabbits, squirrels and a large selection of birds) congregating to sup from its trout-inhabited waters.

While it's not as wild as the fells of neighbouring Cumbria, and is a touch too far inland to enjoy coastal views, this part of the north-west has its own unique charm. Moreover, it's ideally placed for a bit of rural relaxation with the possibility of evening trips into town for a bit of a knees up.

Stanley Villa Farm, Back Lane, Greenhalgh, Preston, Lancashire PR4 3HN 01253 804588
campingbugs.co.uk

✻ There are 24 pods and 12 tent pitches (only available during summer). Campfires permitted; firewood available to buy. Each pod comes with 2 beds and is fully insulated. Two children (or 3 small children) would also fit in a pod, but you would need to bring additional airbeds/roll mats. Guests have 24-hour access to the Lakeside Lodge, which has a kitchen with complimentary teas, coffees, a kettle, microwave, toaster, fridge/freezer, 3 newly fitted wet rooms with toilets and showers, plus a large common room. Power sockets are available in the lodge for hairdryers and charging phones. The lake hosts Rainbow, Blue and Brown trout up to 12lbs and fishing lessons are available to campers.

✻ The Forest of Bowland AONB is a beautiful stretch of rugged, unspoiled countryside covering 312 square miles: perfect for gentle walks, mountain biking, birdwatching and scenic picnics. Lytham St Annes is a charming conurbation most famous for its golf course: a beer festival is held every September and the annual Lytham Proms take place by the town's charming windmill. Morecambe Bay is not too far away either, and then, of course, there's Blackpool, just a 15-minute drive away.

✻ The Eagle & Child (01253 836230) offers a fantastic selection of traditional pub grub. The 'real chips' are highly recommended (particularly since the spuds are grown on Stanley Villa Farm!). The Ashiana (01253 836883) is a superb nearby Indian restaurant. And if you don't mind the 15-minute drive, there is a range of dining options available in Lytham. Try Bosco (01253 733799) for Italian food.

✻ Open all year except Dec and Jan.

✻ Pods £47 per night (except Saturdays and school holidays when they're £56) – based on 2 sharing. Additional occupants £3. Dogs £5.

the hideaway at baxby manor

There's many a way to toast a marshmallow. Some give it a brief wafting over the flames, warming it to a pleasant softness but never daring risk its skin. Others plunge it headlong into the furnace, blackening the outer shell like an overcooked roast potato and melting the inside to a sweet and sticky goo. We all have different tastes and, provided you adhere to the general ethos of loving the great outdoors, The Hideaway at Baxby Manor is the kind of site that caters for every appetite. True, their 'no noise after 11pm' policy means party animals aren't welcome, and the narrow entrance lane keeps the big-boy motorhomes away, but for everyone else this is a real camping playground with families lazing by the campfire, cyclists retracing Le Grand Depart, walkers enjoying the space of the countryside and history buffs nipping across to the old centre of York, this place has the full range of flavours.

Set in the grounds of 14th-century Baxby Manor on the edge of quaint Husthwaite village, this is a hideaway worthy of its name. Approached down a single-lane track with trees on either side, the six-acre meadow has around 40 regular pitches plus, on the south-east edge of the site, glamping accommodation in the form of a number of luxury bell tents and eco-pods, alongside which Ings Beck quietly flows – separated from the campsite by a flank of trees. The bell tents are furnished with proper double beds, lanterns, cooking wares, a kettle and wooden outdoor furniture, and the more permanent-looking eco-pods – sort of akin to a hobbit's Yorkshire holiday home – have futon-style beds inside hexagonal wooden walls. There are three eco-pods in all: two doubles and one that is large enough for a family of four.

In the centre of the site, opposite a young but flourishing orchard, is the main facilities and reception building. The timber structure is home to all the ablutions and a handy shop selling the all-important marshmallows, while some days of the year a friendly local called Emma tows in her trusty retro caravan, 'Liza-Jane' to sell her home-baked goods from its doorstep.

Since the year it opened The Hideaway at Baxby Manor has consistently received awards for its eco-credentials and it's easy to see why – everything the site does falls thoughtfully within their strict green criteria. By the time you leave, though, the greenest thing in your mind will be your own unquenchable envy – jealousy of all those campers who aren't yet heading home.

The Hideaway at Baxby Manor, Baxby Manor, Low Street, Husthwaite, York, North Yorkshire YO61 4PW 01347 666079 baxbyhideaway.co.uk

---

❀ Three eco-pods and several luxury bell tents. You need to bring your own bedding for both. No cooking facilities in the eco-pods, but a gas stove in the bells, along with cooking equipment. Firepits provided (firewood £6 per bag or you can bring your own). A heated timber amenity building houses showers and disabled facilities. There is a drying room, pot wash and food-preparation room, fridges and freezers, shop selling essentials and local food stuffs, plus a book-swap for all. Near the entrance, there's a large games area with exercise park and children's play equipment. There's also an adult-only quiet area, aptly named 'The Sanctuary'.

❀ It's a 5-minute walk from the campsite into the ancient village of Husthwaite, one of many local settlements that appeared in the Domesday Book. There's a village tennis court along with a pleasant pub – the Plum (01347 868007). Elsewhere, it's 3 miles to Shandy Hall (01347 868465), former home of picaresque novelist Laurence Sterne, and a little further to Byland Abbey (01347 868614), one of the greatest early Gothic buildings in England, left in ruins since the 16th-century dissolution of the monasteries.

❀ During the school holidays and every weekend during term time, a vintage caravan ('Liza-Jane') arrives, serving daily breakfasts (8–11am), amazing home-baked cakes and proper coffee. At certain peak times of the year Liza also rocks up for an evening BBQ or posh hot dogs and gourmet hot chocolate. When she's not around, try Andrew Thornton, the village butcher, who visits on Saturday mornings at 10am – you can hire a tripod from the site and grill on site on your own campfire (£5 for the duration of your stay).

❀ Open April–Nov.

❀ Bell tents from £60; eco-pods from £40.

humble bee farm

Humble Bee Farm, Flixton, Scarborough, North Yorkshire YO11 3UJ 01723 890437
humblebeefarm.co.uk

❋ No less than 16 Big Chief Wigwams, 3 bell tents, 4 yurts and regular grass camping pitches during summer – plus 3 onsite cottages if you're visiting with folks who don't do camping of any kind. A children's play area includes a fireman's pole, slide, swings and a climbing bridge. Optional extras include a firepit with wood available to hire each night. Two shower blocks; a central one includes a kitchen area, 1 disabled-access shower, toilets, showers and baby-changing. The facilities behind reception include a laundry, washing-up area and further showers and toilets. The onsite shop supplies basics as well as local sausages and bacon at busy times. There is a duck pond, various animals and kids can see Farmer Percy on his rounds. Happy free-range hens peck about the farmyard.

❋ A section of the 70-mile Yorkshire Wolds Way runs along the site, and you can follow the path for about 7 miles to the small seaside town of Filey and its large sandy beach. Alternatively hop in the car and whizz to the nearby seaside resorts of Scarborough, Bridlington or Whitby, all within an easy distance.

❋ The Foxhound Inn (01723 890301) in Flixton is 1½ miles down the road and comes highly recommended for its huge portions of pub grub. The Filey Deli (Belle Vue Street) boasts the best cupcakes in town and is a good place to stock up for a picnic on the beach.

❋ Open all year.

❋ Wigwams £10–£28 per night per person; yurts £50–£100 a night (midweek), £50–£130 a night (weekends); bell tents £80–£95 a night.

As you bounce along the bumpy track and Humble Bee Farm comes into view, it quickly becomes clear that this is going to be a special place to stay. Hidden away in a tranquil valley among the Yorkshire Wolds, the farm's surroundings are edged with the vibrant colours of bellflowers, harebells and mignonette – wild flowers planted as part of the farm's commitment to conserve wildlife and promote biodiversity. It gives a natural feel to what is an appropriately eclectic site, home to wigwams, bell tents and four fabulous nomadic yurts.

While there are no age barriers to enjoying a stay here, owners John and Julia Warters have turned part of their farm into something of a children's paradise. Pygmy goats, sheep and cattle join the free-range chickens and guinea fowl wandering around and a handful of Aylesbury ducks dabbling on the pond. At busier times of year there's also the opportunity to learn about the farm through special events and themed weekends. This is all, of course, accompanied by the exciting prospect of camping inside a wigwam – all of which are heated and come with mattresses and an outside BBQ and picnic table.

But it's not just kids who will enjoy a stay here. The largest 'Big Chief Wigwams' can sleep a family of five with ease, while bell tents and yurts each sleep four. Though well-equipped, all options can be ramped up by booking 'full glamping' packages, which include every extra, from a bottle of bubbly to a locally sourced breakfast pack and campfire. Toasting marshmallows is, after all, an ageless activity.

There are plenty of activities beyond the children's playground to keep everyone busy. Signposted walks around the farm encourage exploration of the local countryside and the Wolds Way National Trail borders the southern perimeter of the land. Then there are the beaches of nearby Filey, Scarborough and Whitby, which are all within driving distance, and the vast North York Moors National Park, which opens up another world of hiking altogether. The question is, where to start?

pinewood park

Yeehah! Camp Pinewood goes one better than other tipi sites, offering cowboy shacks and Wild West wagons, too. It's easy to see why it's a favourite spot for kids. But over the years it's seen a curious transformation. Not just the westernification of its glamping getup, but also a host of other wonderful camping options, so that the cowboy-friendly caboodle now accompanies several other camping options, including a no-frills tenting field with fabulous views over the Yorkshire Wolds. The pre-pitched tipis, meanwhile, are equipped with futons and cube beds, rugs and outside picnic benches, and have the luxury of electricity (so not exactly the cowboy lifestyle), while the shacks, cabins and wagons come with double beds and modern furnishings, complete with toasters, kettles, fridges, microwaves and heating.

For families, it's a perfect escape. Kids disappear off into the wooded area at the bottom of the site, which has paths weaving around the trees and is perfect for hide-and-seek or Cowboys and Indians, while a great little gift shop at reception sells Wild West toys for little and big kids too.

And it's this flip-side to the location that brings a surprising adult appeal. Outdoor weddings and private events are all catered for (and ever growing in demand) while its enviable location draws in those seeking handy accommodation on the outskirts of Scarborough. It's just a two-mile walk to the centre of town, which enjoys a sandy bay, a crumbling old castle and an historic spa – it's also home to Yorkshire's Sealife Centre aquarium. For those looking for a holiday on the Yorkshire Coast, there really are few more well-appointed spots.

Pinewood Park, Racecourse Road, Scarborough, North Yorkshire YO12 5TG 01723 367278 pinewoodpark.co.uk

❀ Twelve modern tipi tents, 2 Woody's Western Wagons, 4 Cowboy Camping Shacks, 1 Cowboy Camping Cabin, 1 Luxury Camping Lodge and regular camping open all year for tents, campervans and caravans. Tipis are on raised wooden decks, fully carpeted and furnished with a double and 2 singles, storage, an electric heater, light and electric sockets. Woody's Western Wagons feature fixed beds (1 double and 2 singles), lighting, an electric heater, small fridge, kettle, toaster and microwave. Cowboy Camping Shacks sleep families of 4, with a double and 2 singles and all the same furnishings, plus a table and 4 stools are provided on the covered veranda. The Luxury Camping Lodge is the most sumptuous option, with a double and bunk beds, similar furnishings, plus luxury bedding provided and a welcome pack. All electricity is metered and each unit has a picnic bench out front. There's a modern shower and toilet block and al fresco washing-up sinks.

❀ A 2-mile footpath takes you into Scarborough. The quieter of its 2 blue flag beaches is at North Bay, where you'll also find the Sealife Centre (01723 373414).

❀ For great fish and chips or breakfast with local fishermen, head for the Harbour View Café on Scarborough's West Pier.

❀ Glamping and camping mid March–mid Nov.

❀ Tipis £80 per night; Cowboy Shacks £90; Woody's Western Wagons £90; Cowboy Camping Cabin £90; Luxury Camping Lodge £125 (includes bedding). One night stays incur a £5–£10 surcharge. Two free child places in most of the Glamping accommodation.

long valley yurts

Long Valley Yurts, Low Wray Campsite, Ambleside, Cumbria LA22 0JA 01539 733044
luxury-yurt-holidays.co.uk

❀ Three 16-ft yurts on the shores of Windermere (sleeping up to 5 each) and 3 18ft yurts (sleeping up to 6 each) on Whitworths Meadow about a 5-minute walk to the shore. All linen supplied. A fully equipped kitchen including gas hobs; lighting and fairy lights are solar-powered. Immaculate showers and loos are a step away, plus a washing-up area and laundry room with a washing machine and tumble dryer. An adventure playground will keep the kids entertained and you can launch non-powered craft into Windermere from a beach on the site.
❀ Activities offered by Long Valley Yurts include climbing, canoeing, abseiling, ghyll scrambling, mountain and bushcraft, paddle boarding and mountain biking (from £25 for a half-day). Sail, windsurf or waterski on England's largest lake with Windermere Outdoor Centre (015394 47183) or cruise the waves in style with Windermere Lake Cruises (01539 443360). Otherwise you might like to seek out Grizedale Forest for some buzz à la bicyclette, from family-friendly tracks to the taxing North Face Trail. Bikes can be hired at Grizedale Mountain Bikes (01229 860369).
❀ The Drunken Duck Inn (01539 436347) rightly has a reputation for serving some of the best pub food in Britain, and is only a couple of miles away. Lucy's of Ambleside (01539 432288) is a deli with its own café/restaurant and sells delicious if expensive ingredients for campfire dinners. There's also an onsite shop selling the basics.
❀ Open March–Nov.
❀ Yurt prices start from £199.

Tucked away on the quieter western shore of Windermere you'll find the delightful rambling estate of Wray Castle, once the summer abode of a young Beatrix Potter. Nearly 50 years ago the National Trust turned the grounds into what is now one of Cumbria's loveliest campsites, with pitches in fields, pitches (and pods) in woods, pitches right on the lake shore – a real somewhere-for-everyone place. But still there was something missing. 'What about', cried people who wanted to stay there in a yurt, 'people who want to stay there in a yurt?'

Now, with the arrival of Long Valley Yurts, you can, and what a great job they have done too, by adding a collection of traditional yurts decorated with furniture, rugs and lanterns that conjure up a vision of old Marrakech. Each has a wood-burning stove for which firewood and kindling is provided and, should it rain, you can curl up smugly snug with your nearest and dearest or rifle through the games chest and beat them at Monopoly or a similar board game on offer. When bedtime comes, everyone can forget the arguments about which player really won and drift off to sleep gazing up through the skylight at the constellations in the starry sky above.

But it's not all lying back and thinking of Orion. The owners are more than happy to organise a host of activities to get your teeth into – literally, in the case of the bushcraft course. Trained instructors will take you rock climbing, abseiling, ghyll scrambling, mountain-walking, mountain-biking, Ray Mears-ing or canoeing (you can paddle from right outside your front door, down the Blelham Beck which borders the glamping field, and out on to Windermere itself).

England's largest lake is, naturally, a Mecca for lovers of all kinds of aquatic pastimes, with local companies offering a chance to try out sailing, waterskiing, and windsurfing. Or, if that's all a bit too much, you can always hop on to one of the many cruisers that chug relentlessly back and forth over the water.

Finally it's worth knowing that Long Valley Yurts have another site in the Lake District – at Great Langdale, beneath the mighty Langdale Pikes, and a third in the heart of the Peak District, a stone's throw from the grandeur of Chatsworth House and the beautiful Edale Valley. Here at Low Wray, Barny of Wanderlusts Gypsy Caravans (see p.192), also shares some space, keeping a few of his more stationary gypsy wagons.

eskdale

The Lake District is arguably the most beautiful corner of England. With a combination of picture-perfect villages, sensational lakes and glorious green dales, this remarkable region is surely the perfect retreat for any camper. Described by romantic poet William Wordsworth as "The loveliest spot that man hath found", it's hard to disagree, especially on a clear Cumbrian day.

Tucked away down a narrow country lane, Eskdale can be found in one of the Lakes' more secluded pockets. Run by the ever-friendly Sara and Martyn, the eight acres of flat, well-maintained grassland are backed by tall trees with a tranquil stream snaking past, and as well as generous regular camping pitches, it has no less than 10 camping pods set among the trees. The pods are well looked after and very cosy, each sleeping either three adults or two adults and two children. Made with locally sourced timber and insulated with sheep's wool, they provide a basic comfort whatever the weather.

Eskdale may be part of the colossal Camping & Caravanning Club, but it has a welcoming, friendly atmosphere and is a genuinely lovely place to camp. Above all its location couldn't be better. The site is ideally placed for reaching the impressive Wasdale Fells or climbing England's highest mountain, Scafell Pike. There's also one of the most beautiful train journeys in England on your doorstep, the Ravenglass & Eskdale Railway – a historic, narrow-gauge railway that carries passengers through seven miles of spectacular scenery on an unforgettable 40-minute ride.

Eskdale Camping and Caravanning Club Site, Boot, Holmrook, Cumbria CA19 1TH 01946 723253
campingandcaravanningclub.co.uk/eskdale

✻ Ten camping pods, a camping barn (sleeps up to 8) as well as regular camping pitches. Shower/toilet block, laundry room, inside and outside dishwashing areas, pay phone and drying room. Onsite shop selling local produce, ales, camping equipment, and daily essentials. A 14ft enclosed trampoline, swings, and a woodland adventure play area.

✻ The list of things to see and do in the Lake District is endless, so here are some of the closest options. The small, scenic village of Boot is just a few minutes' walk away. After crossing the 17th-century packhorse bridge, you can visit one of very few remaining 2-wheel water mills at Eskdale Mill (019467 23335) and take the 'Millers Tour' to learn about Cumbrian life, its industry and its people. The secluded Japanese Garden at Eskdale Green is one of the jewels in Cumbria's horticultural crown. Following years of neglect, the garden has been lovingly restored and now displays some vibrant Japanese maples, thickets of bamboo and dainty little bridges. Finally the Ravenglass & Eskdale Railway (01229 717171) is a wonderfully nostalgic way to take in the spectacular scenery.

✻ Only a short stroll away is the family-run Brook House Inn (019467 23288). Voted West Cumbria's pub of the year, this traditional tavern serves fine British food and a wide range of local ales. Or try The Woolpack Inn (01946 723230), a charming traditional Cumbrian pub with a sleek new downstairs dining room that serves gourmet wood-fired pizzas. Onsite catering options also available.

✻ Open all year (except late Jan and early Feb).

✻ Camping pods £44.50 per night. Camping Barn £140 per night. Regular backpacker camping from as little as £6.55 per night.

inside out camping

The Borrowdale valley, located south of Keswick, at the foot of Derwentwater, pretty much encapsulates all that's best about the Lake District. Apart from the odd small hamlet, this dramatically beautiful landscape (National Trust-owned for the most part) is the preserve of traditional hill farms, two of which have gone into partnership with glamping provider Inside Out Camping. Two more bucolic sites it's difficult to imagine. At the main glampsite, Hollows Farm, down a roughish but driveable track at the lovely riverside hamlet of Grange, there are three rustically-furnished yurts, which each comfortably sleeping four. The farm operates its own campsite, but Inside Out's yurts are high up the slope of the secluded woodland field, away from the tents, and all guests co-exist happily, sharing the farm facilities.

Three miles down the road, at Seatoller Farm, there are two more yurts, set in their own private field by a babbling river with a plunge pool. Pick your location, or go for an Inside Out lucky dip – either way you're in for a back-to-nature treat in one of the Lakes' loveliest valleys.

Inside Out Camping, Hollows Farm, Grange-in-Borrowdale, Keswick, Cumbria CA12 5UQ
07791 184271 insideoutcamping.co.uk

❀ Six separate, secluded yurts plus regular tent pitches. The yurts (4 at Hollows Farm, 2 at Seatoller Farm) each sleep 4, though an airbed is available if necessary for a fifth person. On both sites, toilets and cold water are a couple of minutes away, though it's a longer walk for a hot shower at the respective farmhouses (5 minutes for Seatoller, 10 minutes at Hollows Farm). It's National Trust land, so no campfires, though each yurt has a BBQ.

❀ This is great hiking country – there are gorgeous valley and riverside walks straight from Hollows Farm, while Seatoller Farm is handier for more serious climbs up Scafell Pike, Great Gable and others. The major town of Keswick (market days on Thurs and Sat) is 5 miles up the road (there's a regular bus), and there are cruise-launch piers all around nearby Derwentwater (017687 77263) so you can leave the car at the campsites for the duration.

❀ Grange Bridge Cottage Tea Shop (01768 777201) is perfect for riverside teas and lunches, and no less than Prince Charles is a regular visitor to the Flock-In café and farm shop at Rosthwaite's Yew Tree Farm (01768 777675). The best valley pub is the Riverside Bar at the Scafell Hotel (01768 777208), also in Rosthwaite; you can walk from either site, but take a torch for the journey back.

❀ Open Easter–end Oct.

❀ Mon–Fri or Fri–Mon bookings £285–£360; whole week £385–£520.

lanefoot farm

Lanefoot Farm, Thornthwaite, Keswick, Cumbria CA12 5RZ 01768 778097 stayinthornthwaite.co.uk

❀ Shepherd's huts, camping pods and a vintage caravan plus regular camping pitches. Campfires allowed. Good clean loos (3M, 3F) and 3 bright showers, washing-up area, drying room. Tiny shop sells basics and meats. There can sometimes be minimal traffic noise.

❀ Walks include popular local routes up Grizedale Pike and Skiddaw, while there's also mountain bike rental and world-class trails at Whinlatter Forest (01768 778469). You can tour nearby Derwentwater by way of the regular launches (01768 772263) and Mirehouse & Gardens

(01768 772287) provides a great day out for the family.

❀ Try a mini pub crawl in Braithwaite village, where the Royal Oak (01768 778533), Coledale Inn (01768 778272) and Middle Ruddings (01768 778436) are all good bets for drinks and food – in a roughly ascending order of quality. There's also the General Store for basics, organics and local beers. If you scrub up nicely enough, there is classy dining on Bassenthwaite Lake at the Pheasant Inn (01768 776234).

❀ Open March–Nov (also open for New Year Dec/Jan).

❀ Shepherd's Hut and standard camping pods from £38–£43 per night. Family pod from £44–£49 per night. Vintage caravan £50 per night.

There's been a campsite in this little corner near Keswick since the 1960s, but it had rather fallen into decline until wonderfully amiable owners Gareth and Helen took over Lanefoot Farm and injected it with new life (and a few free-range chickens). The result is a revitalised site that has the sort of facilities you'd be happy to eat your dinner off and a collection of new glamping options for those folks like us who call themselves 'campers' but are suspiciously lacking in a tent. The site's pods and shepherd's huts, tucked beneath the trees, offer a comfortable yet still affordable alternative – where you bring your own gear and sleeping bag, yet benefit from insulation, electricity and double-glazed doors – while a vintage 1960s caravan is a perfect luxury hideout for folks who love a touch of the old-school style.

For campers and glampers alike, the atmosphere here at Lanefoot Farm is one of laid-back relaxation combined with a few necessary practicalities. There's a little shop on site, chickens roaming free and a friendly, chatty atmosphere, while cyclists in particular are impeccably well catered for – the site is bang on the C2C route and there are mountain-bike trails a-plenty in the nearby Whinlatter Forest.

For most people it is this proximity to all things outdoors that makes for such a winning site. Arguably there are few spots in the Lake District National Park as beautiful as this little north-west corner, midway between Bassenthwaite Lake and Derwentwater. You can make things easy for yourself by touring Derwentwater by way of the Keswick Launch, which runs all the way around the lake, and Bassenthwaite is home to Mirehouse & Gardens, which makes for a good family day out. Pub quiz devotees will also be excited to learn that Bassenthwaite Lake is technically not only the Lake District's only lake (the rest are 'waters' or 'meres') but that it is also home to the vendace, Britain's rarest fish. Next question please, landlord!

scales plantation

Much has changed on the remote hill farms of the Lake District. Shepherd's huts have been overtaken by the hum of quad bikes; bucket and pail replaced by mechanical milking parlours, and tractors rumble where carts once rolled. The timeless beauty of the place, however, is as awe-inspiring as ever and to most it seems life has never changed. The sheep-dotted fields and stone walls rise and fall in an almost alpine landscape, augmented by waterfalls and picturesque villages. In short, it's the perfect place for an off-grid glamping getaway, and in the forest-clad grounds of Scales Farm, views, ewes and a cosy place to snooze are all guaranteed.

Scales Plantation, a 13-acre woodland in a corner of the working farm, is a campsite that owes a lot to the changing world of agriculture. Here the retired shepherd's huts of yesteryear have been thoughtfully placed by the trees, spruced up with luxury furnishings and equipped for more modern-day nomads looking to camp in style. While the Wilson family still rise at the crack of dawn to tend their thousand-strong herd of sheep, campers can stay tucked up in bed warmed by the glow of a wood-burning stove. When the kettle whistles, drag yourself from under the duvet, throw open the door and stroll to the kitchen shelter, kitted out with everything you need to whip up a hearty breakfast. A rustic wooden dining area, also in the shelter, is perfect for days when it's too wet to sit out around the campfire.

There are three shepherd's huts on site, along with two safari tents and a pair of creamy bell tents beside their own sturdy wooden cabin. Each of the accommodation types are within their own 'camp', all with their own private bathrooms. All the camps are in a forest clearing with a central firepit and solar lighting that leads you to a composting loo and, whichever you favour, you're guaranteed spectacular views across to Skiddaw, Bowscale Fell and Carrock. There are plenty of good footpaths nearby, while the nearby A66 from Keswick to Penrith provides speedy access to the centre of the National Park.

Scales Farm, Berrier, Penrith, Cumbria CA11 0XE
01768 484779 scalesplantation.com

❋ Three shepherd's huts, 2 bell tents (with wooden cabin) and 2 safari tents, each accompanied by a compost loo. Each shepherd's hut has a double bed at one end and bunk beds at the other (bedding and linen provided). Bunk beds can be folded down into a seating area if not required. Huts are fully insulated and have a wood-burning stove with logs provided. Solar power supplies lighting and a socket for appliances under 300w. Each camp includes an outside dining area and a BBQ pit, but there is also a kitchen/dining shelter with a wood-burning range cooker, gas hob, fridge and sink. The bathroom shelter leads off from the dining area and has hot water and a wood-burning stove warming the room. Towels, but not toiletries, are provided.

❋ Walk from the site through Greystoke Forest or take on the more strenuous 9.5-mile 'Glendermakin Round', starting from nearby Mungrisdale. Caldbeck-based Savvy Mountain biking (0800 6123576) can deliver bikes and safety equipment to the site and also offer guided rides. Nearby Keswick, situated between Skiddaw and Derwentwater, is the focal point of the North Lakes and boasts the quirky Pencil Museum (01768 773626) and one of England's most innovative theatres (01768 774 411). Stop off on the way at Castlerigg Stone Circle.

❋ The campsite can organise delivery of local produce from Hesket Newmarket Village Shop (01697 478229) if needed. The Mill Inn (01768 779632), at the foot of Souther Fell and Blencathra in the unspoilt village of Mungrisdale, serves excellent food, as does the brilliant Boot & Shoe (01768 483343), which overlooks the village green in Greystoke.

❋ Open all year.

❋ The camps can be booked for a long weekend (Fri–Mon), a 4-night midweek stay (Mon–Fri) or a full week's stay. Prices start at £250 for a midweek off-season break.

wanderlusts gypsy caravans

"What a shame my house doesn't move." It's not the kind of thing you hear often as returning holidaymakers struggle to find the keys to the front door. Yet after a long weekend at Wanderlusts, it's precisely such a statement that's likely to ring around the cavernous rooms of your bog-standard, normal home. Set up by Barny Maurice, who ran away to the circus aged 16 and lived with fellow trapeze artists for over 20 years, Wanderlusts is a true on-the-road experience that puts campers in control of their new home and shows them the romantic, bohemian lifestyle of living on the move. The creek of wooden wagon wheels, the breeze in your hair and the ever-changing country backdrop – his creation is far more than your everyday idea of 'glamping' (although you can, if you prefer, opt to stay in one of his static gypsy caravans at Low Wray campsite, p.180).

The experience begins from the moment you arrive, meeting at a local pub or car park to be picked up by a traditional, bow top gypsy caravan that Barny has painstakingly restored. Clambering up to the cabin, guests can not only prep themselves for a few nights beneath the stars as they rattle down the road, but also have the chance to take the reigns and bring the caravan to life under the trusted power of a gorgeous Shire horse.

The journey – as well-run as it is unique – takes passengers through the quiet country lanes of Cumbria, stopping along the way at pre-organised camps that Barny has arranged over the years with various local landowners. Each of the camps is specifically chosen – in wildflower meadows, nestled by a private tarn, lake or millstream – and all have toilets and space for an open fire. One, which Barny describes to us as an 'island field', is perched between diverging waters with a flank of tall trees on the third side, while another spot rests on the banks of a kidney bean-shaped lake where campers can wild swim in the waters, gazing up at the rising Pennines all around. The spaces feel authentic, wild and untainted – which is precisely Barny's aim – and once you are set up with a roaring fire, you are left entirely to the sounds of wildlife, water and utter peace and quiet. Whether you trek with your trusted steed or ride in the beautiful cocoon of the gypsy caravan, all options build on Barny's indefatigable knowledge of nomadic life – knowledge he is all too happy to share. One thing is for certain: you won't think of 'home' in the same way again.

Wanderlusts Gypsy Caravans, High Barn Cottage, Edenhall, Penrith. Cumbria CA11 8SS
07706 361685 wanderlusts.co.uk

❁ The Gypsy Caravan is mostly made of wood, lined on the inside with a warm fabric and covered in traditional canvas. There is a double bed (with bedding) plus sleeping mats for children (or adults) for which extra sleeping bags and/or bedding is needed. There's a gas hob, kettle, frying pan, pots, cups, plates, cutlery, wash bowl, water container and cupboards for storage. For lighting there is a wind-up torch, candles and 12v lights. For washing-up and bathing you'll have to heat water over the campfire – Barny can provide help if you need it. All camping spots will have either a compost or outside loo close at hand.

❁ For those on the move, the itinerary is somewhat set in stone so that you and the horse can get to certain points at specific times for rest and relaxation, plus arrive at each camping spot in time to explore and enjoy splashing in the stream, visiting the watermill, drinking in the pub or swimming in the lake – depending on which spot you are stopping at. For those staying in the static gypsy wagons at Low Wray, there's a wealth of activities in the local area. A lakeshore path leads to the National Trust's Wray Castle (01539 433250), which is great for families, with a range of activities, including the new Peter Rabbit Warren, and boats go from there to the Lakes Visitor Centre at Brockhole (01539 446601).

❁ There are lots of pubs en route, but it's worth bringing some supplies and planning a few meals that you can cook over the campfire for maximum enjoyment. On the road, there may be the possibility to buy seasonal produce, from eggs to cakes and homemade jams. At one camping stop-off, the neighbouring watermill, where toilets are also found, has an excellent tea room and facilities. You can often buy fresh goats' milk or a freshly baked loaf warm from the oven here too.

❁ Tours available all year.

❁ Three-night weekends or 4-night midweek breaks from £180 per night for up to 2 people; children £20 per night extra; additional adults £30 per night.

hesleyside
huts

The Charlton family have lived at Hesleyside since 1343, when Edward Charlton first cobbled together a rough pele tower of stone and turf. Over time it grew both in physical size and political stature. First, to a large square tower with a cluster of dwellings at its foot, then to a two-storey fortified house, until, by the 18th century, Hesleyside Hall was one of the grandest mansions in Northumberland, with sweeping grounds, avenues of ageing trees and an elegant Palladian façade. Today, in the greenery that lies beyond, the Hesleyside estate offers modern-day glamping, which is similarly distant from the wattle-and-daub days of yore. Although rustic and simple from the outside, these reclaimed oak huts are a real treat for any camper who likes their comforts – proper luxury hideaways in the grounds of a Northumbrian manor.

Stepping through the door of one of Hesleyside Hall's oversized shepherd's huts you are greeted with a scene far beyond the reality of any humble sheepherder. Almost a cottage on wheels, these abodes are more like cosy groundsmen's lodges in the gardens of the mansion than the rickety work cabins of 19th-century shepherds. All have electricity, a fully furnished kitchen and a toasty wood-burning stove, while the 'all you need'

collection of matching crockery, kitchen utensils, toiletries and lanterns means guests are impeccably well catered for. The layout, too, is luxurious, with a plush en suite bathroom, whopping king-sized bed and a cosy twin bunk. The newest (and largest) of the huts, in the style of a petite wooden chapel, even has a second-storey mezzanine bedroom, giving extra space for a huge bronze bathtub downstairs.

Despite the beautiful interiors, it's the surroundings which are the stand-out feature of this campsite – not only the romantic estate grounds but also the countryside around. Seemingly endless forest stretches west towards glistening Kielder Water, where you can go sailing, kayaking and water-skiing, while the surrounding North Tyne valley is famed for its excellent mountain biking and walking trails. Hesleyside Huts also sits within the 'Northumberland Dark Sky Reserve', so is an excellent spot for stargazing – which is made easy by the binoculars, telescope and informative books laid on for you in each hut. When you're done picking out constellations you can slip back into the warmth of your hut, a cocoon of comfort beneath the starry Northumberland skies.

Hesleyside Huts, Hesleyside, Bellingham, Hexham, Northumberland NE48 2LA 01434 220068
hesleysidehuts.co.uk

❊ Three shepherd's huts and a fourth, secluded hut in the style of a New England pioneer chapel. 'Bracken' hut has a raised double bed plus a pull-out child's bed. 'Heather' has a drop-down bunk suitable for a child and an enclosed bed area with a king-sized bed. A fold-down table optimises space in the living area and the large pull-out drawer houses everything guests need for a night of stargazing. 'Bramble' boasts a king-sized 4-poster bed and a separate bunk room, while 'Holly' (the chapel) sleeps 2 in the mezzanine, while downstairs there's a large bathtub with shower. Huts have electric plugs and lighting; pots, pans, cooking equipment, crockery and cutlery; a dresser and mini Belfast sink; and a wood-burning stove, oven and hotplate. Campfires are permitted and an initial supply of logs, kindling and fire lighters is provided. There is an en suite bathroom in each hut with eco-friendly loo, handwashing basin and power shower. Bedding is included.
❊ Within the grounds, the North Tyne has excellent fishing that can be arranged by talking to Anna. Beyond, the Kielder reservoir (0845 155 0236) and surrounding forest has endless walking trails, off-road mountain biking, sailing and other watersports. You could also take a trip to Hadrian's Wall (01914 405720), a short drive south, and historic Vindolanda (01434 344277), while lovers of gardens, stately homes and *Harry Potter* will have heard of Alnwick Castle & Garden (01665 511100).
❊ Optional breakfast baskets can be organised in advance and cooking facilities in the huts include a tripod, trivet, cauldron, griddle and skillet. The Cheviot (01434 220696), a 5-minute drive away in Bellingham, and The Pheasant (01434 240382), slightly further, in Stannersburn, serve good food.
❊ Open all year.
❊ Fri–Sun stays £100 per night, otherwise £90 per night. Additional tents £15 per night. Two-night minimum stay.

the bells of hemscott

For sheer dramatic beauty, the stunning Northumberland coast takes some topping. The wind-buffeted beaches along this unspoiled stretch of the north-east coast seem to go on forever. With endless wildlife ponds, undulating sand dunes and the boundless, shimmering blue of the perma-choppy North Sea, there couldn't be a more fitting setting for a spot of wild camping.

Introducing The Bells of Hemscott – a pop-up experience open for several weeks in the summer that combines the thrill of off-grid camping with a few choice comforts. Located on affable host Alison's working Hemscott Hill Farm, The Bells offers acres of open space in which guests can savour the great outdoors. And yet, there's an intimacy here that belies Hemscott's proximity to the sprawling peaks and valleys of the Northumberland National Park.

There's a shepherd's hut and, of course, a good number of pre-erected, fully furnished bell tents in Hemscott's so-called Canvas Village. The location of the Village changes every year depending on farming activities, but you will never be more than a 15-minute walk from the beach. Alison can also accommodate a number of tents in the Wild Camping area on large spacious pitches next to the open sandy beach, too.

Hemscott is a well and truly off–grid camping experience. The meagre facilities that exist are basic but perfectly clean and functional – think compost loos and eco (but hot) shower huts. But, hey, places like this don't need much in the way of window dressing. And when you throw in the fact that there's still a hot tub for glampers to hire, you'll find that plenty of inquisitive eyebrows begin to start raising!

On the farm, Alison has a number of rare breeds, and campers can, by appointment, interact with some of the animals, including walking the amiable alpacas or visiting the Kune Kune pigs, the hens and ducks. There's always plenty of opportunity for small animal handling for the kids, too.

Beyond, meanwhile, the Northumberland coast is deserving of the accolade 'a walker's paradise'. Venture in any direction from Hemscott for countless spectacular strolls – from the fossil-strewn beach at Hauxley to the many ancient castles that dot the northern stretch (Northumberland has more castles than any other county in England, don't you know). And as dusk descends, stoke up the campfire back at Hemscott and enjoy the dazzling sunsets as they yield to the twinkling light of infinite stars under the UK's darkest night skies.

The Bells of Hemscott, Hemscott Hill Farm, Widdrington, Morpeth, Northumberland NE61 5EQ 07876 344509 thebellsofhemscott.co.uk

❀ Twelve bell tents and a shepherd's hut in the Canvas Village, plus 30 regular camping pitches next to the dunes. Off-grid facilities include compost loos, showers and a kitchen/washing-up hut. Bell tents are furnished with a futon or double air-bed and you need to bring your own bedding; the shepherd's hut has a double sofa bed. Firepit included outside. Campfires permitted in firepits and BBQs must be raised off the grass.

❀ Easy access to the golden sands stretching from the 2 beaches at Amble in the north to Cresswell Beach in the south. Explore this 7-mile stretch of Druridge Bay Country Park via the Northumberland Coast Path. The farm is also on the stunning Coast Castles National Cycle Route 1, an easy path that takes in Warkworth Castle (01665 711423), Bamburgh Castle (01668 214515) and Dunstanburgh Castle (01665 576231). You can hire bikes from Breeze Bikes (01665 710323) in Amble.

❀ The Widdrington Inn (01670 760260) and The Plough (01670 860340) in Ellington are both decent locals, serving not only a changing selection of ales but also hearty pub grub.

❀ Open selected dates July and Aug.

❀ Bell tents from £80 per night, shepherd's hut £95 per night, camping from £20 per night. Two-night minimum stay (3 on bank holidays).

roulotte retreat

Take one chilled-out yoga teacher, one sleepy wildflower meadow and a clutch of handcrafted roulottes (gypsy-style French wooden caravans) and you have one seriously relaxed escape. This is where Audrey Hepburn would have glamped had she known about it, and owners Avril Berry and Alan Fraser are rightly proud of their caravans of love. Children are a no-no, but many guests actually turn out to be parents looking to put a bit of wild romance back into their lives.

The roulottes are not so much rustic as resplendent, reminiscent of a luxury train suite with smooth hardwoods, delicate carvings and lush furnishings. One of Avril's ancestors was a renowned painter of gypsy caravans, and his talents have been passed on, with real attention to detail woven into each roulotte. No two are the same. Karlotta is all art deco flourishes, Moorish influences and Celtic imagery, while Devanna takes her cues from India. What they all have in common is that they are very lush, extravagant and seriously sexy.

The roulottes are sprinkled around the lochan in the wildflower meadow, where the two resident geese sometimes wander in to have a swim. Afterwards they stretch out their wings to take in the sun as guests stretch out their own limbs, relaxing on their decks while having a barbecue or lounging by the communal campfire. Most people don't even make it out to explore the famous Borders scenery of rolling hills and snaking rivers that so entranced Scotland's greatest ever writer, Sir Walter Scott.

The Retreat also has a cottage, which comes with its own small gypsy bowtop in its woodland garden, while in the meadow you'll find Zenaya and Gitana – complete with their own eco hot tubs, hidden away in secret for exclusive bathing for two under the star-scattered Scottish skies. Roulotte Retreat also has a 1950s wooden studio with a large covered deck wrapped around a Scots Pine Tree woodland. It's perfect for gatherings, celebrations, weddings or workshops and has consequently seen Avril start to offer regular yoga sessions. So you can do your Cobra, Half Moon pose, or Downward-facing Dog as the sun casts its warm, morning shards through the canopy. Now that's glamping!

Roulotte Retreat, Bowden, Melrose, Scottish Borders TD6 0SU 0845 0949729 roulotteretreat.com

❀ Seven roulottes, each with an en suite with powerful shower and separate modern toilet; also a cooker and wood-burning stove, a retro BBQ outside, plus independent heating. Avril offers yoga lessons, either one-to-one or in a group. Ask about yoga holidays and other workshops (art, photography, creative writing, etc).
❀ The charming market town of Melrose is just 4 miles away, with its gloriously ruined abbey (01896 822562) – famously where the seminal Scottish king Robert the Bruce's heart was buried after it was taken on Crusade. Melrose also offers boutique shops, delis, cafés and riverside walks. If staying in June, be sure to visit the Borders Book Festival. Between Melrose and Roulotte Retreat, the Eildon Hills are ideal for adventurous walks, with peaks to climb and plenty of trails to explore. The St Cuthbert's Way, which goes from Melrose to Lindisfarne, runs nearby the site and leads down to the River Tweed.
❀ Breakfast hampers with local produce can be organised – just order in advance when you're booking. Historic Burt's Hotel (01896 822285) in Melrose has a great bar within with over 90 whiskies and is also home to an award-winning restaurant serving up the best of Borders produce. The Townhouse (01896 822645), just across the road, is run by the same family and offers a brasserie and a restaurant serving Borders lamb, salmon and trout as well as excellent vegetarian fare. Marmions Brasserie is a tasty bistro for lunch, dinner or their very tasty meze. If you are coming as a group, you could even hire your own chef for your stay – ask Avril for details. Avril also organises street food-style trucks and chefs for wedding celebrations.
❀ Open all year.
❀ Prices £95–£135 per night in low season to £105–£165 per night in high season – depending on which roulotte you choose. Eco hot tubs are an additional fee.

runach arainn

It's difficult to understand how an island so small can offer so much. If you're looking for a remote retreat, then Arran is unquestionably ideal – the salty wind slapping your cheeks as you ferry across the Firth of Clyde will remind you of that. But no matter how much the island may draw you in with its isolation, the character and friendliness of the place will quickly make it feel like home. By the end of the week you will know the route to the beach as if it were the school run and The Lagg Inn's landlady will have a tab running in your name.

Right at the southern end of the 19-mile-long island, where the mountains give way to hills and rocks turn into long sandy beaches, you'll find Runach Arainn. An unashamedly luxurious glamping site, it's a relatively new enterprise for the island, but it seems to be going down a storm. On the banks of Kilmory Water and within the grounds of an old rectory built in the 1600s, it's the perfect starting point for the island's 21st-century charm offensive. It has just three yurts, each accompanied by a private bathroom with an excellent shower and composting loo. Each sleeps up to six people, but they also work nicely as a romantic break for two, with a deep, double bed alongside two double futons that you can use either as sofas or as fold-out beds for larger parties. In harsher weather the likes of a toasty wood-burning stove and a hefty stack of logs allows you to create your own cosy cocoon, while the circular crown at the top of the yurt lets you peep out at the constellations above.

It's Andrew and Pippa who really make Runach Arainn what it is, though. Having moved to the island in 2013 from their office-job lives in middle England, their clear passion for the area has already made them more island-hardened and knowledgeable than erstwhile billy goats. The romantic rural setting they have created – with ducks and hens wandering around the site and a forest garden in the early stages of growth – is enough to keep you occupied for hours, while, off site, farm tracks lead you quickly into Kilmory Parish, with its homely pub and exceptional beach. When the tide is out the sands open up to a vast, flat pancake and, across the wavy waters, Ailsa Craig pokes from the sea – a distant volcanic island mined for its rare type of blue granite that lays claim to two-thirds of the entire world's curling stones.

Runach Arainn, The Old Manse, Kilmory, Isle of Arran KA27 8PH 01770 870515
runacharainn.com

❀ Three fully insulated yurts each featuring a double bed plus 2 double futons for additional guests. They're fully equipped with all you need, including a wood-burning stove for heat and cooking, plus all utensils and crockery. Private bathroom with a shower and a composting toilet. Outside there is a firepit, more cooking wares and a picnic bench. Shared pot-washing and laundry facilities a short walk away. Chickens, ducks, geese and bees provide a near-constant supply of fresh eggs and honey.

❀ It's a 15-minute walk to Torrylinn Beach, a vast sandy space when the tide is out with excellent views across to Ailsa Craig in the distance. From the yurts you can gain access directly to forest farm tracks and footpaths, which are ideal for a casual stroll or some light mountain biking (for something more serious you could try cycling the entire 60-mile circuit of the island). You can hire bikes from the Arran Adventure Company (01770 302244), which also offers a wide range of other outdoor activities. Inland, you could visit the Neolithic standing stones of Giants Graves in Whiting Bay or the stone circle at Machrie Moor. The island also boasts a staggering 7 different golf courses – so, if you bring your clubs, there's one for every day of the week!

❀ It's a 10-minute walk to the nearest restaurant, at the Lagg Hotel (01770 870255), where landlady Mary is accompanied by friendly staff and an excellent chef. It's great for an evening meal but also well worth an afternoon stop for their homemade scones! The nearest shop is a local store in Blackwaterfoot, which is a 15-minute drive away.

❀ Open all year.

❀ Prices start at £200 for a short break (3–4 nights) in low season.

bramble bield

In the shadows of some of the bloodiest battlefields in Scotland and perhaps the nation's finest castle lies a sleepy wee gypsy caravan retreat that could not be further from the days of clashing broadswords and bloodcurdling war cries. Bramble Bield may be firmly in William 'Braveheart' Wallace country, just a catapult's hurl from Stirling Castle and the omnipresent Wallace Monument, but life here is a relaxed affair, with just a trio of little brightly painted traditional caravans tucked between the meadow and beech, ash, and hawthorn trees.

The site's three caravans, Rowan, Bramley and Holly, are the real bow-top wooden caravan deal – indeed Bramley has been here or hereabouts since the 1920s. They are cosy and compact inside, with luxurious bedding, original Queenie stoves and tea- and coffee-making facilities making up for the lack of space (you are allowed to pitch a two-person tent by each caravan too). An outdoor patio set accompanies each caravan and there is a communal campfire to toast marshmallows over. Neat touches include the breakfasts provided in the amenities block of the old stables, with freshly baked bread, croissants, pastries and eggs from the hens on offer. After a morning feast fit for a warrior, beyond the tranquil world of Bramble Bield those epic battlefields and castles await.

Bramble Bield, Powis House, Stirling FK9 5PS
01786 460231 bramblebield.com

❈ Holly sleeps 2 adults and 2 children, Rowan sleeps 2 adults and comes with Bramley, at no extra cost. Bramley has a futon/settee and can be used as a small sitting room or bedroom for 2 children. Amenity block in old stables with shower, toilet and kitchen facilities. Campfires permitted and stoves inside each caravan (stove coal for sale). For the caravan dwellers, a shower and wash basin is provided. There's also a separate eco-friendly compost toilet and separate urinals. Adjacent field with sheep and goats – handy for entertaining kids.
❈ The city of Stirling is only a few miles away. The star of its charming, cobbled old town is Stirling Castle (01786 450000), perhaps the most striking and certainly one of the most historic castles in Scotland. From the ramparts, you can see the mighty Wallace Monument (01786 472140) a few miles away – worth visiting in its own

right both for the views and to discover more about Wallace, one of Scotland's greatest heroes. A drive or cycle away, the Trossachs are a range of rugged hills and mountains that form a sort of Highlands in miniature. Wee Ben A'an (461m) offers perhaps the best effort-to-reward ratio of any hill in Scotland.
❈ Stirling has some decent restaurants, but the area's best is at the Lake of Mentieth Hotel (01877 385258). Dine outside or in the conservatory restaurant and enjoy epic views out across the eponymous lake and moor-covered hills. The whisky bar here is superb, while their Port Bar serves simpler meals with an emphasis on fresh, local produce. In the Trossachs, Callander boasts Mhor Fish (01877 330213), a brilliant all-in-one chippie, fishmonger and simple seafood restaurant – it's not to be missed!
❈ Open March–Oct (other special occasions considered).
❈ From £140 in low season for a 2-night midweek stay, to £160 in high season (July–Aug). Breakfast included.

comrie croft

Before the Act of Union and the birth of the modern British state, many Scots lived on crofts, smallholdings of land where communal living was the norm. In the heart of deepest Highland Perthshire this communal ethic has been re-created at Comrie Croft. Run by a co-operative of likeminded, environmentally aware individuals, this is no mere campsite. Yes they take tents, but they've also got Norwegian *katas*, an onsite Tea Garden and a superb bike shop, the latter handy for exploring the network of trails that snake off up the Croft's wooded hillside.

Four of the five *katas* lie up in the forest, where the most secluded pitches are located, each with their own campfire. A sort of Scandinavian tipi, the *katas* come complete with a wood-burning stove and a large sleeping area strewn with animal skins. It's not exactly super-chic glamping, but it is supremely cosy. There is little need to leave the Croft. Down by the car park is a superb camp store, which stocks everything from fluorescent camping pegs to free-range eggs and fresh local meat. The bike and walking trails wind their way up the hill and are very tempting – though you may want to brush up on your mountain-biking technique first at the site's very own skills park. On a busy day – and most weekends are busy – Comrie Croft buzzes with life, just as the traditional crofts once did all over this charmingly scenic corner of Highland Perthshire.

Comrie Croft, Braincroft, Crieff, Perthshire PH7 4JZ
01764 670140 comriecroft.com

❋ Five *katas* and 32 regular camping pitches. Campfires allowed. Solar and wind-powered amenities block with toilets and good showers (including disabled access seat). Excellent camping shop. Blue and red mountain trails and skills park with bike-hire and helmets available. A network of marked walking trails as well as picnic areas. Chicken feed available in the store for feeding the chickens.

❋ The high land beyond the boundaries of the Croft is tough-going, but opens up sweeping views of Strathearn for adventurous and well-equipped hikers and bikers. Perthshire is excellent for walking, and there's a map detailing local routes both posted and available for sale in the Croft store. The Croft lies between the neat, Highland Perthshire towns of Crieff and Comrie, with their characterful high streets, parks and walks. The Auchingarrich Wildlife Park (01764 679469) is a handy family attraction just south of Comrie.

❋ The onsite Tea Garden at Comrie Croft is excellent, with croissants or bacon rolls for breakfast and the likes of salmon bagels with cream cheese and salad for lunch. The vintage crockery is a nice touch, as is the wooden deck. The cakes are homemade and huge! Comrie has a reasonable chippie (07514 678833) and the Royal Hotel (01764 679200), which has a characterful hunting lodge-style bar in the main hotel and a more pub-style drinking den just outside, with real ales and whiskies. Their restaurant, under the smooth hand of chef patron David Milsom, features succulent Perthshire lamb and salmon, among other delights.

❋ Open all year.

❋ *Katas* £179 per weekend (Fri–Sun), £75 per weeknight. Ten percent discount for those who come without a car.

loch tay highland lodges

Scotland is one of the world's great active destinations, its mountains, rivers and lochs being brilliant for getting right in among the great outdoors, and campsites don't come any more ideal for adrenaline junkies than Loch Tay Highland Lodges. At the foot of the site they offer both canoeing and kayaking, boat hire, fishing and thrilling RIB rides from their very own Loch Tay marina, while they also rent out mountain bikes. Then there is the new hiking path that links up with the epic trail that goes up Ben Lawers which, at 1,214 metres, is Perthshire's highest mountain and higher than any mountain in England and Wales. Just a scenic drive or cycle along the banks of Loch Tay, the River Tay's whitewater charms also await.

Loch Tay offers various glamping options, from cosy, heated wigwams to domes and woodland cabins. All have access to a excellent washing facilities, a common room and a fully equipped camper's kitchen (the premium wigwams boast their own cooking facilities). The domes sit in the old camping field, enjoying views over Loch Tay and back towards the mountains. A childrens' playground, putting green, communal campers' room with large TV and leather sofas and the waterfront Loch-side bistro complete the facilities on this seriously adventurous site.

Loch Tay Highland Lodges, Milton Morenish Estate, By Killin, Perthshire FK21 8TY 01567 820323 lochtay-vacations.co.uk

❁ Wigwams, glamping domes, woodland cabins and lodges. A brand new facilities block with showers, toilets, private bathroom (which can be rented), drying room, launderette and vestibule with wood-burning stove. Excellent campers' kitchen with additional living area with sofas and large TV. The marina offers kayaking, canoeing, RIB rides, sailing, fishing and boat hire. Other activities such as quad biking and mountain biking. There's also Wi-Fi, a play area, putting green and disc golf. Campfires allowed in the firepits provided.

❁ A path leads directly up towards Ben Lawers, a serious mountain ascent that should only be tackled by the well-equipped and suitably skilled. The Lawers range also boasts a number of other Munros (mountains over 3,000ft/914m). At the other end of Loch Tay lies the Scottish Crannog Centre (01887 830583), providing a fascinating insight for all the family into how people lived around Loch Tay thousands of years ago. Nearby Aberfeldy is the centre of the River Tay's whitewater activities – from where Splash (01887 829706) run trips.

❁ The onsite family-friendly Loch-side Bistro offers a wide variety of dishes, along with loch views on a wooden deck overlooking the marina. Bar meals, pizza and pre-ordered packed lunches can all be ordered. Elsewhere, The Bridge of Lochay Hotel (01567 820272) boasts creative cooking using local produce with the likes of baked haggis bon-bons with a turnip velouté or Scottish ribeye with chorizo. The hotel also has a bar that is well-stocked with local ales and Scottish whiskies.

❁ Open all year.

❁ Wigwams from £25 per adult per night and £10 per child. Glamping domes from £35 per adult per night and £10 per child. Lodges from £245 per night, woodland cabins from £220.

aviemore glamping

Aviemore Glamping, Eriskay, Craig Na Gower Avenue, Aviemore, Inverness-shire PH22 1RW   01479 810717
aviemoreglamping.com

❀ There are 4 glamping pods, each sleeping 2. Each has its own en suite wet room as well as tea- and coffee-making facilities. All pods come fully equipped with bed linen, towels, cups, glasses (plus complimentary tea, coffee and milk). BBQ area outside with a firepit (firewood is available to buy).

❀ The Cairngorms National Park boasts endless scenery and outdoor activities. Take the Cairngorm Funicular Railway (01479 861261) up 3,500ft to get a true sense of its scale. It's also home to the wonderful Cairngorm Reindeer Centre (01479 861228) where, under the supervision of trained staff, you can feed, stroke and walk among these friendly animals. Aviemore is the outdoor capital of Scotland, with everything from skiing and gorge walking to loch kayaking and winter mountaineering on offer. The site is just 10 miles from the ski slopes, with regular shuttle buses every hour.

❀ You can order a delicious cooked breakfast on site for just a fiver. Elsewhere, The Old Bridge Inn (01479 811137) serves a sophisticated gourmet menu, and Ben Macduis Inn (01479 811754) does decent, reasonably priced meals, especially fresh fish dishes.

❀ Open all year.

❀ From £60 per pod per night – 2-night minimum stay.

Think skiing and what places spring to mind? Val d'Isere? Whistler? St Moritz? A resort in the heart of the Scottish Highlands might not evoke the glamour of such illustrious names, but Aviemore in Inverness-shire is the destination of choice for a great many of the UK's piste artistes. High on the northern fringes of the vast Cairngorms National Park, Aviemore is a year-round base for outdoor enthusiasts of all persuasions. From kayaking on Loch Morlich to tackling the mighty Munros of Britain's highest, coldest, and snowiest mountain range, this unspoiled landscape is a veritable smorgasbord of epic features just waiting to be explored.

And while there's a refreshing lack of exclusivity about Aviemore, accommodation at the resort proper often falls on the pricey side. What a treat then to find Aviemore Glamping – a hassle-free pod site in the grounds of a charming B&B. Situated in the shadow of Craigellachie Hill, Aviemore Glamping is the perfect base for your outdoors adventure holiday – near enough to the slopes to indulge in a spot of après-ski, but a safe enough distance from the hustle-and-bustle of the resort to enjoy a bit of peace. It's a compact and stylish town-centre site, offering excellent-value accommodation,

with four ingeniously-designed timber pods that can comfortably sleep a couple on a fold-out double bed. The immaculately maintained shower/wet room in each one is a true feat of ergonomics and has a real sense of space and light thanks to the massive circular window. Most importantly, these cosy cabins stay nice and toasty in those teeth-chatteringly cold Highland evenings, and are kitted out with all the kit-and-caboodle you could need, including bedding, cutlery and utensils. There aren't any cooking facilities, but you need only nip across the gravel path for your full-hearted Scottish breakfast, courtesy of your full-hearted hostess Pat. Okay, it's not exactly 'roughing it' under canvas, but you are provided with a communal firepit so that you can toast marshmallows and stare at the pristine blanket of stars. And that's what it's really all about, isn't it?

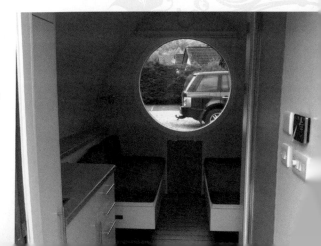

ace hideaways

Ace Hideaways, Auchnagairn, Dunphail, Forres, Moray IV36 2QL 01309 611729 acehideaways.co.uk

✳ Three bell tents for families or groups, a shepherd's hut for couples and a handful of regular camping pitches. Woodland showers and composting loos, plus a well-equipped woodland camp kitchen. Campfires are permitted. The shepherd's hut features a full-size double bed, wood-burning stove and a gas ring cooker. Bell tents feature mattresses and bean bags but they're sparsely furnished and you'll need to bring your own bedding (sleeping bags available for hire). A host of activities are offered on site, including whitewater rafting, tubing, kayaking, canyoning, cliff-jumping, disc golf and paintball.

✳ The campsite is around 2 miles from the Logie Steading Visitor Centre (01309 611378), which is a good starting-point for finding information on the local area. It's about 12 miles to the Moray coastline, with its vast sandy beaches and fishing villages. To the south lies the Cairngorms National Park (01479 873535), an established spot for serious walking and cycling, with lots of marked trails.

✳ The reception shop stocks a few camp essentials plus hot drinks and chocolate bars. The closest place to get a good, freshly prepared lunch made is at the café at Logie Steading (01309 611733), 2 miles away (they serve great cakes and coffee too). If you'd like a decent pub lunch or supper, maybe with a walk on the beach, the Kimberley Inn (01309 690492) in Findhorn is a great choice.

✳ Open April–Oct.

✳ Bell tents: adults from £11.25; children from £7.50. Shepherd's hut from £55 per night for a couple. Dogs £5.

Ace Hideaways is a remarkable place. Enigmatic in many ways, it avoids any one single definition and makes its name as a campsite – or hideaway – for every kind of escape. The setting is one of serenity and peace, with clearings in the woods with off-grid glamping accommodation and basic camping pitches, yet its adrenaline-pumping, heart-thumping adventure arm lends an altogether different atmosphere – one of white-water action and paint-balling fun.

The type of holiday you're after, of course, is entirely up to you. Those heading north for a quiet escape are blessed with the remoteness that Morayshire affords. The mature trees of the site reach across one another to enclose you in a cocoon of quiet, while miles of footpaths, rivers and empty spaces remind you of what makes this part of Scotland so special. Adrenaline addicts, meanwhile, can make their way down to the River Findhorn, don a lifejacket and hurl themselves in, either by canoe, kayak, raft, or by simply plunging in on one of their cliff-jumping sessions.

Facilities-wise, things are similarly eclectic. There are three large bell tents, furnished with mattresses or bean bags, and a shepherd's hut for two that is more equipped for a luxury glamping break. Each have their own clearing in the woods, while compost toilets and gas-heated showers blend seamlessly into the woodland surroundings. There's also a communal cooking area, with campfire pits, utensils and sinks, along with a huge log table and stools, crafted out of a giant tree.

There's plenty to do locally. The Findhorn Valley is known for its rich woodland and spectacular gorges. You can, in fact, walk the two miles from the campsite to Logie Steading Visitor Centre where there's ample information on the wildlife of the area. Not that you really need to go that far. Couples in the shepherd's hut can peer from its tiny windows like birdwatchers in a hide, while everyone else can creep around quietly with binoculars to hand. You'll be surprised just how many creatures frequent the site – a sign of just how subtle and eco-friendly this place is.

dry island

Opportunities to take a holiday on your very own island don't come around very often. Uniquely situated on Scotland's wilder-than-wild west coast, Dry Island sits in the tranquil Badachro Bay, whose warm Gulf Stream waters attract a plethora of marine wildlife. Current owner Ian is a direct descendant of the family who have lived, fished and farmed on this tiny Scottish island for centuries, and he still fishes for shellfish here today. After a few days of breathing in the fresh sea air and exploring the nearby hills and beaches, you'll come to realise just why the Mackenzie clan has never left.

Dry Island has accommodation in the form of two self-catering cottages and the cosy Badachro Bothy — a large, secluded wooden cabin with decking and undercover outdoor seating that enables guests to enjoy the woodland and sea views whatever the weather. Step inside and you'll find bunk beds, sofa beds, a heater and your own private shower and WC.

What next? How about a Shellfish Safari? In summer you can join local skipper Ian on his traditional creel fishing boat and help him to haul langoustines, lobsters, crab, octopus, starfish, scorpion fish and beautiful shells from

Badachro Bays' crystal-clear waters. Some of Ian's shellfish ends up on plates at Gordon Ramsay's restaurants, but you can sample this delicious fresh food for yourself, so why not take a bucket home for tea? Also, keep your eyes peeled for the wonderful array of wildlife: dolphins, porpoises, seals, otters and sea eagles are all known to frequent the bay. Beyond the island, you can climb the giant sandstone Torridon Mountains, as well as discover Skye, Rona and the Inner Hebrides. But why would you leave? Ian and his other half Jess are the undisputed 'King' and 'Queen' of Dry Island and its only permanent inhabitants. They have even given the island its very own currency (the crab), flag (a crab and Saltire) and legislation, such as "all visitors must smile". And with a big bucket of fresh seafood for tea, you'll have every reason to.

**Dry Island, Badachro, Gairloch, Ross-shire IV21 2AB
01445 741263 dryisland.co.uk**

❉ Badachro Bothy is a secure wooden cabin with a bunk bed (small double and single) and a comfortable double sofa bed. It has its own private shower, WC and heater, and linen and towels can be hired. Decking and an undercover outdoor seating area with a firepit along with woodland and sea views. The Bothy is close to your own play-park with slides, swings and football goals.

❉ The loch is circled to the south by the dramatic Torridon Mountains, including the 3,300-ft-high Beinn Alligin and its slightly smaller sibling, Slioch (3,215ft). Treks here involve some of the best ridge-walking in Scotland, with scrambles to suit both beginners and the more advanced. At 90 minutes' drive away, Inverness is the nearest large town – the primary city of the Highlands, with a great location by the River Ness at the northern end of the Great Glen. In summer it overflows with tourists intent on monster-hunting at nearby Loch Ness, but it's worth a visit in its own right or to take a cruise on the Moray Firth in search of the inlet's famous bottlenose dolphins.

❉ A stone's throw from the shores of Gair Loch, the Badachro Inn (01445 741255) is perfect for unwinding after a day on the hills. It's a cosy pub with a varied menu that changes daily, with many dishes featuring locally caught seafood. The fantastic Independent Inverness Farmers' Market is held in the city centre on the first Saturday of every month and is well worth a visit for the freshest produce.

❉ Open all year.

❉ From £50 per night in low season to £65 per night in high season. If Badachro Bothy is booked in conjunction with The Old Curing Station holiday cottage there is a 5% discount.

wheems
organic farm

Wheems Organic Farm, Eastside, South Ronaldsay, Orkney KW17 2TJ 01856 831556 / 07400 542026 wheemsorganic.co.uk

❀ Wooden camping bothies, a 14-ft yurt and regular camping pitches. BBQs and small campfires allowed. Two showers and 3 toilets in a wooden building by the bothy. Campers' kitchen with 2 small electric cookers with lovely wooden surfaces, including tables and chairs. There is also a washing machine, fridge, freezer and a hairdryer, plus books and games for the kids. Each bothy is provided with bedding (optional), a heater, water-container, chargeable lamp and hot water-bottles. The yurt is more lavishly furnished, with beds, bedding, blankets, towels, candles, lamps, a wood-burning stove and firewood for your stay.
❀ Off site, make a pilgrimage to the small Italian chapel on Lamb Holm, which was built by and for the Prisoners

of War while they were here during World War II. Like most things in the Orkneys, it's a simple and unassuming place, but beautifully done. An even shorter walk away, you'll find a pristine sandy beach, which is also the starting-point of a fabulous 10-mile circular hike. Alternatively drive 20 minutes to Kirkwall, where you can wander the labyrinth of stone-paved streets or visit the gallery and co-operative craft and gift shop in St Margaret's Hope (01856 831587).
❀ Wheems' own fruit, veg and eggs are on sale in their shop. Alternatively, Creel (01856 831311) in St Margaret's Hope is widely regarded as one of Scotland's best restaurants.
❀ Open early April–end Oct.
❀ Bothies £35; yurt £50 for one night, £45 per night for multiple nights.

Not for nothing did the poet and novelist George Mackay Brown say that the Orkney imagination was haunted by time. There's something other-worldly about the Orkney Islands, where there has been a human presence for thousands of years (the living in places like Skara Brae, the dead in the Neolithic burial chamber of Maes Howe). The land has been smoothed over by the prevailing winds, and the resulting views are of rolling hills and water between the 70 islands that make up the archipelago. The dun hills are like the patternless tweed of a geography teacher's jacket and the sky can be everything from broody to menthol-clear.

Many visitors arrive on the short ferry hop from Gills Bay, between Thurso and John O'Groats, at the charming little port village of St Margaret's Hope. From here it's a couple of miles over the hill to Wheems Organic Farm. Owned and run by Mike Roberts and family, the campsite has a simple and fitting ethos: to keep things small, simple and eco-friendly but, most of all, to share the beauty of this ethereal setting with all who choose to visit.

Along with regular camping pitches, Mike has constructed four solid wooden bothies, insulated with sheeps' fleece and with long double-glazed doors that open on to a deck overlooking the bay. Mike's daughter Islay,

meanwhile, has poured her efforts into a new, Mongolian-style yurt, with beautiful latticework walls and a toasty wood-burning stove in its centre. Between them they have something for every visitor. Campers and caravanners can pitch in the meadows, visitors travelling light can bunk in the wooden bothies, while those wanting the full comforts of a double bed and proper furnishings can head straight for the yurt.

There are toilets, showers and a communal kitchen housed alongside the farm buildings, and, if the hens are playing ball, fresh eggs are available along with other homegrown produce. BBQs and small campfires are permitted, depending on wind direction and the possibility of spark damage to neighbouring tents. Dogs are welcome as long as they are kept on leads. All in all, there's no better place from which to discover this far-flung and very special part of the UK.

Koa Tree Camp, see page 24

Find and book your perfect glamping holiday

To instantly check availability for hundreds of glamping options and book at the best price, visit

www.coolcamping.co.uk

Acknowledgements

Glamping Getaways, second edition

Series Concept and Series Editor: Jonathan Knight
Editor: Martin Dunford
Assistant Editor: James Warner Smith
Contributors: Shelley Bowdler, Andrew Day, Sophie Dawson, Keith Didcock, David Jones, Martin Dunford, Jonathan Knight, Robin McKelvie, Sam Pow, Amy Sheldrake, Clover Stroud, Alexandra Tilley Loughrey, James Warner Smith, Richard Waters, Dixe Wills, and Harriet Yeomans.
Designers: Kenny Grant, Diana Jarvis
Proofreader: Leanne Bryan

Published by: Punk Publishing, 81 Rivington Street, London EC2A 3AY

UK Sales: Compass IPS Limited, Great West House, Great West Road, Brentford TW8 9DF; 020 8326 5696; sales@compass-ips.co.uk

All photographs included in this book have been licensed from the authors or from the campsite owners, except the following: pp14–15 © Emma Woodhouse; pp18, 19 © Richard Tamblyn; pp40, 42 © Sophie Munro; p43 © Matt Sweeting Photography; p82 © Jenny Hardy; pp92–93 © Rebecca Douglas; pp94, 95 © Robert Canis; p108 © Carl Lamb; pp136, 138–139 © Ben Radford; pp140, 141 © Gavin Taylor Photography; pp192, 194–195 © Saskia Stewart; p193 © Russel Colman Photography; pp202, 204, 205 © Helen Abraham/Philip Heywood; pp216, 217 © Max Branter.

No photographs may be reproduced without permission. For all picture enquiries, please contact enquiries@coolcamping.co.uk

Map © MAPS IN MINUTES™
Reproduced with permission.

Front cover photograph Ivy Grange Farm, Suffolk © Carl Lamb, ambientLight

The publishers and authors have done their best to ensure the accuracy of all information in *Glamping Getaways*, however, they can accept no responsibility for any injury, loss or inconvenience sustained by anyone as a result of information contained in this book.

Punk Publishing takes its environmental responsibilities seriously. This book has been printed on paper made from renewable sources and we continue to work with our printers to reduce our overall environmental impact.

We hope you've enjoyed reading *Glamping Getaways* and that it has inspired you to visit some of the places featured. The accommodation in this book represents a small selection of the glamping sites approved and recommended at **www.coolcamping.co.uk** where you can also leave your own reviews, search availability and book camping and glamping accommodation.